MIRACLES

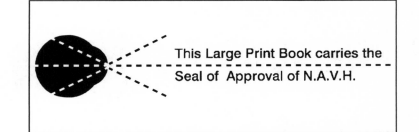

This Large Print Book carries the
Seal of Approval of N.A.V.H.

MIRACLES

A 52-WEEK DEVOTIONAL

KAREN KINGSBURY

THORNDIKE PRESS

A part of Gale, Cengage Learning

GALE
CENGAGE Learning·

Detroit • New York • San Francisco • New Haven, Conn • Waterville, Maine • London

LIBRARY OF CONGRESS CATALOGING-IN-PUBLICATION DATA

Kingsbury, Karen.
  Miracles : a 52-week devotional / by Karen Kingsbury. — Large print ed.
    p. cm. — (Thorndike Press large print inspirational series)
  Portions of this book have been adapted from A treasury of miracles for women, 2002; A treasury of miracles for teens, 2003; A treasury for friends, 2004; A treasury of adoption miracles, 2005; A treasury of Christmas miracles, 2001, 2007.
    ISBN-13: 978-1-4104-2230-9 (hardcover : alk. paper)
    ISBN-10: 1-4104-2230-5 (hardcover : alk. paper)
    ISBN-13: 978-1-59415-316-7 (softcover : alk. paper)
    ISBN-10: 1-59415-316-7 (softcover : alk. paper)
  1. Miracles—Anecdotes. 2. Large type books. I. Title.
BT97.3.K53 2010
231.7'3—dc22   2009036544

Published in 2010 in arrangement with Faith Woods, a division of Hachette Book Group, Inc.

Printed in Mexico
2 3 4 5 6 7 13 12 11 10

Dedicated to

Donald, *my Prince Charming,*
Kelsey, *my precious daughter,*
Tyler, *my favorite song,*
Sean, *my happy heart,*
Josh, *my determined one,*
EJ, *my chosen child,*
Austin, *my miracle boy,*
And to God Almighty, *who has — for now — blessed me with these.*

CONTENTS

WEEK 1.
NEW YEAR'S EVE

SCRIPTURE READING:
PSALM 124

Flee the evil desires of youth, and pursue righteousness, faith, love and peace, along with those who call on the Lord out of a pure heart.

2 TIMOTHY 2:22

For the first time ever, Mia Parsons and her friend Tanya Andrews were going to celebrate New Year's Eve with a hundred thousand people at the all-night party preceding the Tournament of Roses Parade in downtown Pasadena, California. Excitement didn't come close to describing the way the two seventeen-year-olds felt.

The girls had joined a group of a dozen friends who were part of their local Young Life club. They'd have plenty of fun without drinking, but Mia was a bit concerned about Tanya. The girl was a new friend and had just started attending Young Life. Mia wasn't completely sure of how crazy Tanya might get.

As darkness settled and people walked the parade route, the Young Life group laughed and danced to street music. One small man walked past them, then turned, set his eyes on Mia, slowly approached, and handed her a yellow sticker that read: "Jesus loves you."

"Thanks," Mia said. "He loves you, too."

The man nodded and smiled, then walked away.

"That was strange," Mia said to Tanya.

Tanya shrugged. "It's New Year's Eve. You never know who you'll meet. Let's enjoy the night."

As the night progressed, cars cruised the boulevard bumper-to-bumper, barely moving as the riders waved at the people. A pickup truck with two good-looking young men pulled up in front of the two girls.

"Wanna ride?" one of them called out.

"Right!" Mia shouted over the noise that filled the street. "Like we'd take a ride from strangers."

"Oh, come on. We're just circling the parade route. Climb in the back and we'll take you around once."

Mia and Tanya exchanged a knowing glance. At that instant, Steve Simons from their Young Life group stepped in. "What's going on? Do you know him?"

Tanya stepped forward. "Yes. From

school." She shot a desperate look at Mia.

Mia eyed the handsome boys. What harm could come if she and Tanya rode once around the parade route? Traffic was so slow, they could always jump off. "Sure," she replied. "We met them last year."

Steve stepped back. "As long as you know them."

Mia grabbed Tanya's hand and the two girls situated themselves against the rear of the cab and waved at the hundreds of people along the parade route. Mia felt wonderful with the wind in her hair, celebrating the New Year in style. So what if they'd told a small lie.

But after thirty minutes of extreme fun, Mia noticed the crowd was thinning and the parade markers were gone. Then she looked in the cab and saw that the boys were laughing hard and drinking, and empty beer cans were on the floor of the vehicle.

Just then the truck came to a stop at an intersection. "We're leaving Pasadena!" She gripped Tanya's arm. "The guys are leaving with us!"

Suddenly, above the noise to the truck's radio, Mia heard a voice say, "Get out! They're taking you to the beach to rape you."

Panic filled her heart. She had no time to

wonder who had spoken the warning as she glanced ahead and saw that they were about to enter the westbound Ventura Freeway that eventually led to the beach.

"Quick!" she shouted at Tanya. "We're in trouble! Get out!" But Tanya didn't move to jump.

Suddenly the driver sped up and barreled toward the freeway ramp. In a split-second decision Mia decided she'd rather die on the roadway than be raped. *God, help me . . . please!* Then she stood up and jumped.

Mia felt herself sailing through the air and thought she would surely die. Then there was nothing but silence. Cars from all directions came to a screeching halt as her body slammed onto the pavement and slid into the middle of the intersection. None hit her.

A motorcycle policeman saw it happen, called for help, and was instantly at her side. He knew she must have serious injuries. "Don't move," he said, taking her pulse.

Mia couldn't make sense of what was happening as others rushed in to try to help. Nothing hurt. Instead, there was a great sense of urgency. "My friend in the truck! They're going to rape her!"

The officer looked up and saw the truck entering the freeway. Immediately he climbed back onto his motorcycle, flipped on his red lights, and in a few seconds pulled the truck over.

When Tanya got back to Mia, she was crying. "Why did you jump? You could have killed yourself."

"They were going to rape us, Tanya. I heard it. Someone told me they were taking us to the beach."

"Who? I didn't hear it." Tanya's face grew pale as she looked back at the truck where the police were administering a sobriety test. "Mia, I can't believe we were so stupid. Are you okay?"

Mia looked herself over. Her white denim jeans were completely clean and unharmed. She remembered her hands sliding across the asphalt, but her skin was unscratched. There wasn't even any dust to brush off. "I'm fine," she whispered. "Perfectly fine."

At that moment, Mia glanced down at the yellow sticker on her shirtsleeve. "Jesus loves me," she said out loud, then she looked at Tanya. "It was a miracle. That's why that man gave me this sticker. God knew what was going to happen, and he looked out for us."

Tanya reached out and hugged her friend tightly. It would be a long time before the shock of what had happened that night would wear off.

Mia felt the sting of tears in her eyes. "It'll be a New Year's Eve I'll never forget."

How great is the love the Father has lavished on us, that we should be called children of God! And that is what we are!

1 JOHN 3:1

Week 2.
The Littlest Angel

SCRIPTURE READING:
ACTS 27:13–26

Are not all angels ministering spirits sent
to serve those who will inherit salvation?
HEBREWS 1:14

Dr. Deidre Givens was exhausted. After
fifteen years of neurological work in Boston,
the single woman had developed an extensive list of patients and an equally impres-
sive reputation. But Deidre — who found
her strength in a strong faith in God — paid
a price for her success, especially on days
like this.

The hospital had been overcrowded because of the cold weather that January, and
the accompanying increase in illnesses. In
addition to helping tend to the swarms of
people, Deidre had performed several bur-
densome examinations and two tiring sur-
geries.

At home that night, Deidre had just
poured herself a cup of coffee when there
was a knock at the door. *Not now, God.*

Please. I'm tired.

It was nearly nine o'clock, bitterly cold, and snow had been piling up outside. Deidre headed toward the front room. She opened the door. "Yes?" There stood a little shivering girl dressed in a tattered coat and worn-out shoes, perhaps five years old. She was crying and she turned her huge brown eyes up at Deidre.

"Ma'am, my mother is dying," the girl said, her voice choked by the sobs. "Please, could you come? We don't live far."

Deidre felt her insides melt with concern for the child. She had the sweetest, purest voice that cut through Deidre's tired body and caused her to spring into action. She grabbed her coat and her medical bag and took the little girl's hand. Then the two headed into the storm.

Less than two city blocks away, in a section of tenement apartments, the little girl turned into a doorway and led Deidre up two flights of stairs.

"She's in there," the little girl said, pointing toward a bedroom at the end of a narrow hallway.

Deidre moved quickly toward the bedroom and found a woman who was very sick, nearly delirious from a high fever and close to death. A quick listen to her chest told Deidre that the woman was suffering from pneumonia and that her fever needed to be reduced if there was any chance to save her life.

For more than an hour Deidre worked over the woman, soothing her hot, dry skin with compresses and arranging for her to be transported to the nearest medical facility. Finally, when the woman's fever began to subside, she slowly opened her eyes, blinking because of the light. Deidre continued to work tirelessly, sponging her head and trying to cool her body with wet rags.

Struggling to speak, the woman thanked the doctor for coming. "How did you ever find me?"

Deidre smiled. "Your little girl saved your life. I would never have known you were up here otherwise. Thank her. Sweet little child, braving the cold, stormy night and walking the streets until she found me."

A look of pain and shock filled the woman's eyes. "What are you talking about?" she asked.

Deidre was puzzled. "Your little girl," she repeated. "She came and got me. That's how I found you here."

The woman shook her head and her hand flew to her mouth as if she were trying to contain a scream.

"What is it, what's wrong?" Deidre took the woman's hand in hers and tried to soothe her sudden panic. "Your little girl's all right."

"Ma'am . . ." Tears streamed down the woman's face as she fought for the strength to speak. "My little girl died a month ago. She was sick for weeks and . . ."

Deidre stepped back, shocked by the woman's story. "But she knocked on my door and led me here! I held her hand until she showed me where you were."

The woman's tears came harder and she pointed toward a closet in her cramped bedroom. "There, that's where I keep her things since she died."

Deidre walked slowly toward the closet. There was the coat worn by the little girl only an hour earlier hung completely dry. The same shoes sat neatly on the floor.

"These belonged to your daughter?" Deidre's heart pounded. It wasn't possible.

"Yes, ma'am." The woman wiped her wet cheeks with the sleeve of her nightgown.

"The girl who led me here wore this coat and those shoes." Her mind raced, searching for understanding. Then finally it dawned on her that the little girl had to be somewhere in the apartment. But after searching for several minutes, Deidre returned to the sick woman's bedside. "She's gone."

The woman nodded, fresh tears filling her eyes. "I told you. My daughter's dead."

Deidre's heart still pounded, her mind still searched for an explanation. But then it dawned on Deidre.

"It's a miracle." Deidre took the woman's hand and shrugged. "I can't think of anything else to call it."

The woman nodded and suddenly her face broke into a smile, the tears replaced by a strange, peaceful look. "Her angel came back to help me. There is no other explanation."

Deidre nodded, feeling the sting of tears in her own eyes. After the ambulance had taken her patient off to the hospital, she walked home slowly through the snow, pondering the impossible and wondering about life. There was so much she did not understand or know.

Years later, Deidre would tell the story about the little child who, although dead more than a month, had somehow appeared on the steps in search of help for her dying mother. And Deidre would still feel the same sense of amazement she had that cold, wintry evening. She believes with all her heart that medical technology cannot always explain the ways of life.

And to this day she believes the girl must have been an angel. The littlest one of all.

He sends from heaven and saves me, rebuking those who hotly pursue me; God sends his love and his faithfulness.

PSALM 57:3

Week 3.
Heaven's Perfect Timing

SCRIPTURE READING:
MATTHEW 2

Teach us to number our days aright, that we may gain a heart of wisdom.

PSALM 90:12

Her freshman year of college, Amy Baron commuted between college and home so often she became expert at it, even the most difficult stretch of the roadway locals called "the Summit." She had to drive up the steep grade of the Allegheny Mountains on Route 22 before reaching the Summit, with its winding turns and steep drop-offs, where the roadway leveled out at the top of the mountain range. It was extremely dangerous there because without the protection of surrounding mountains, crosswinds made driving treacherous in any weather.

One day in January, Amy walked out of her last class and gazed at the menacing clouds moving in, then whispered a prayer, "God, help me get home safely. Don't let me cross that summit if it's dangerous."

She got in her car and drove the surface streets toward Route 22 in creeping traffic. The clouds looked more dangerous, more ominous, than usual. She felt her stomach churning, then noticed a fast-food restaurant right before her turn onto Route 22.

Suddenly she was gripped by a strong urge to get something to eat. She resisted, thinking it was crucial that she clear the Summit before the storm, but again she was overwhelmed with the desire to eat. But it was two o'clock and she'd eaten lunch. There was no reason to be hungry. But then she felt her skin become hot and tingly and became light-headed. She was prone to bouts of low blood sugar, and her symptoms indicated just that.

Can't I wait, Lord? I have to get home.

Just as she was about to pass the restaurant, a voice rang through the car. "Stop and eat, Amy." She glanced into the backseat, but there was no one there, and the radio was off. A chill ran down her arms. At the last second, she turned and headed toward the drive-through window.

Amy ordered a cheeseburger and then waited, which seemed to take forever. She took her bag and swung out toward the road when another wave of clamminess washed over her. Without thinking, she pulled her car into a parking spot and stopped. She was angry with herself for the delay, but the instant she began eating, the clammy feeling left and her strength returned.

The sky was frighteningly dark as Amy's car climbed the mountainside and snowflakes began to hit her windshield. She drew a deep breath. *Please, God . . . guide me.* As she drew closer to the Summit, the snow began coming in sheets. Fear wrapped its arms around her, and she slowed to leave a safe distance between her car and the one in front of her.

Gripping the steering wheel, Amy came to the top of the Summit. Suddenly, the snow completely engulfed the roadway. She was in the middle of a whiteout, with wind howling in different directions and snow making it impossible to see more than a few feet. She had no choice but to stop, but if a car hit her from behind, even a minor accident could send her through the guardrails, tumbling to certain death thousands of feet below.

One minute passed, then two. Finally Amy saw that the car she was following had also stopped. Glancing back, she could barely see lights stopping behind her as well. More minutes passed, then suddenly the snow cloud lifted and Amy could see that she was the tenth car behind a jackknifed tractor-trailer blocking the road.

Amy took her cell phone and called her parents. "It's Amy. I'm stuck on the Summit. The storm's lifted, but there's a jackknifed semi in front of me. It'll be a while."

Amy's father said, "I heard there's a report of an accident up there. Can you see it?"

"All I can see is the truck." The traffic began to inch forward, and Amy peered ahead. The moment she moved past the semi, she cried, "Dad . . . no! It's awful!" There were dozens of cars smashed together, piled on top of one another in the ditch between the two sides of the highway. "I have to stop and help, Dad."

The man in the car ahead of her had already stopped and was running from mangled car to car. Moments later he returned and asked to use Amy's cell phone, calling for ambulances. He looked at her and said, "People are hurt all over. Some of them are dead. A few minutes earlier, and we'd have been in that disaster."

In a few minutes the ambulances rolled in. Amy noticed the crumpled cheeseburger wrapper in her car, and it suddenly dawned on her if she hadn't heeded the voice, hadn't stopped to eat, she might even be dead now. It had taken an extra seven minutes . . .

that God used to keep her from tragedy.

It took nearly three hours for Amy to drive home using a detour route. During that time she pondered the mercy of God and why she had been spared while others died. Why? Then she remembered something her father had told her once. The kindest thing God had ever done was to provide a way to heaven through Jesus Christ. Today simply wasn't her day to go home. It was part of the mystery of God. He knew the reasons why things had happened the way they did.

Thirty vehicles had been involved in the accident, and nearly a dozen people had died. Weeks later, a white cross was erected at the site, and every time Amy passes it, she whispers a heartfelt thank-you to God and remembers the day he used a cheese-burger to save her life.

I trust in you, O LORD; I say, "You are my God." My times are in your hands. . . . Let your face shine on your servant; save me in your unfailing love.

PSALM 31:14–16

Week 4.
A Series of
Miracles
SCRIPTURE READING:
LUKE 1:5–25

I rescued the poor who cried for help, and
the fatherless who had none to assist him.
                                                    JOB 29:12

When Vince Anderson was a high school
sophomore, he told his sweetheart, Sharon,
that he knew how life would go for them.
"I'm going to marry you one day, and we'll
have six kids."

They had known each other since junior
high and Sharon didn't doubt Vince's intentions. "Six is perfect," she told him. "Three
girls and three boys."

Through high school, their relationship
was on and off. Finally it was their senior
year and time for the prom. Despite all their
previous plans to go to senior prom together, both found other dates. The day of
the big dance came and they weren't even
speaking to each other, both silently hurt by
the other's actions.

But after their eyes met on the dance

floor, Vince waited for his chance and met Sharon in the hallway. "Why are we doing this to ourselves? I can't think of anyone but you."

Sharon could feel tears in her eyes. Her heart was thawing fast.

"Remember?" He leaned in and kissed her on the lips. "I'm going to marry you and we'll have six kids."

Sharon's heart leaped when he reached for her hand. She knew she was where she belonged.

"Don't ever let go again, okay?"

Sharon never did. She and Vince didn't look back once, not through college, and not after they married. But despite the plans they'd had for so long, they were unable to have children.

"We've done all we can do," the doctor told them. "Have you considered adoption?"

Sharon and Vince never had. They went home dejected, but that night they prayed for a miracle, that God would fill their house with children the way only he could do. After much discussion, they made a call to a local international adoption agency. They decided to adopt a little girl from China — a place where girls are often aborted because of their gender.

The process was long and arduous, but finally they were matched with a four-year-old girl named Mai Lan. They flew to China and immediately fell in love with her. She had huge brown eyes and a smile that played on her lips despite her shyness.

"We'd like to have many children," Vince said when they met with the director of the orphanage. "Does Mai Lan have any siblings?"

The director shook her head. "Mai Lan is the only girl. We have many other children if you're interested."

Sharon and Vince were, but they decided to adopt only Mai Lan, and when they brought her home they gave her the nickname Molly. For the next two years they savored every moment with their new daughter. Every once in a while she would say something about Mai Lin.

"Is Mai Lin your friend?" Vince would ask.

"She's my sister. My little sister."

"Honey, you don't have a sister."

"I do, Daddy. Her name is Mai Lin."

The couple wondered if maybe Molly was making up the little girl, but the memory remained.

Not quite a year after Molly's adoption, and against all medical understanding, Sharon became pregnant and nine months later delivered healthy twin boys.

On the two-year anniversary of Molly's adoption, they decided to adopt another little girl from China. When they discovered that Molly's orphanage was closed down, they chose a five-year-old named Christine from an orphanage located fifty miles away.

From the beginning, they were struck by the resemblance between Molly and Christine. "It's uncanny," Vince told his wife on the flight home. "They could be the same child."

Molly and Christine were fast friends from the beginning. They talked the same and laughed the same.

"She's my sister, Mommy," Molly said. "Thank you for bringing me my sister."

Sharon felt uncomfortable, but she chuckled lightly. "Of course she's your sister. She's in our family just like the babies. All four of you are brothers and sisters."

But when Christine wound up allergic to wheat and dairy, the same as Molly, Sharon approached Vince. "I want the girls tested; I want their DNA checked." Sharon's hands trembled as she explained the reasons. "What if they really are sisters?"

"It's impossible. You know what the orphanage director told us. Molly had no sisters."

"I know, but what if? Molly's talked about a sister from the beginning." Sharon paused. "I couldn't go all my life without knowing."

Vince agreed, if only to put Sharon's doubts at ease. The couple was together when they got the news that rocked their world.

Molly and Christine were full biological sisters.

The odds were beyond anything anyone could explain, but Sharon contacted the orphanage and found out the story as best as it could be relayed. Apparently the birth mother had three daughters. But when local government officials discovered it, her two youngest daughters were taken away. Christine's original name had been Mai Lin — just as Molly remembered.

The entire situation felt like a series of miracles to Sharon and Vince, a couple who might not have realized any of their dreams if not for a bold move made at the senior prom. It's something they talk about often, when they're not busy running their six children around.

In addition to Molly and Christine and the twin boys, Sharon gave birth to another son and finally a daughter, making the miracle of their lives complete.

Every good and perfect gift is from above, coming down from the Father of the heavenly lights, who does not change like shifting shadows.

JAMES 1:17

Week 5.
God's Ways

SCRIPTURE READING:
GENESIS 30:1–24

They are the children God has graciously given your servant.

GENESIS 33:5

After four miscarriages, Margaret and Bill Jefferson endured a daily sense of loss that was cavernous. They had been married six years and wanted babies desperately. Having tried just about everything, they were running out of medical options.

Finally Bill began praying that Margaret would find a friend, someone who might understand her pain, the desperation to be a mother one day. Not long afterward, Margaret signed up to be part of a book club at her church. There she met a woman who shared Margaret's sorrow of multiple miscarriages.

It was Joanne who asked Margaret if they had considered adoption. Margaret had always pictured their babies coming from her and Bill — not from a stranger. "Is that

34

how you . . . ?"

"Yes." Joanne grinned. "We adopted two sisters, who wouldn't have had a chance otherwise."

"How can you . . . how do you love them as your own?"

"They are my own. If God puts a child in our homes, that child is our own for as long as God desires. They're all on loan, when you think about it."

Margaret let the idea sink in. *All children belong to God. His to give, his to take, on loan for a season.* That night she asked Bill, "Honey, what do you think about adoption?"

"I've thought about it, but guess I've been afraid. I had a teacher who was so excited about adopting a little boy, but the birth mother changed her mind."

"So the adoption fell through. How awful."

"Yeah. She was never the same after that."

"That's why you never brought it up?"

"I guess. Even talking about it makes me think about the possibilities for disappointment."

That part sounded terrifying to Margaret also. But certainly birth mothers didn't change their minds often. "God knows what he's doing," she would tell Bill over the following weeks. "He knows we couldn't stand that kind of loss. Maybe we should look into it a little more."

Finally they contacted a private adoption attorney and shared their fears.

The attorney shared his understanding of their feelings. "It's up to me how I match you up. You can be sure the adoption is almost 100 percent risk-free."

Almost 100 percent. The phrase caught on the edges of Margaret's nerves. The fact was, she and Bill could only pin all their hopes on God. He alone knew what they could tolerate.

Six months after finishing their home study, the attorney called them to his office. He had located a twenty-four-year-old birth mother, who'd given up one other child two years earlier. Her notes in the file explained that she didn't believe in abortion, but she had no interest in being a mother.

The adoption would be open, something the birth mother had requested. Margaret and Bill were fine with that, believing that a woman who had thought things through to that point would be more likely to stand by her decision. Besides, the woman had already given up one child. The odds were as good as they could get.

Months passed and they learned that the

woman's baby was a girl. Aware that their little girl would be coming home in just five weeks, they named her Brianna Suzanne, decorated her bedroom, and counted the days.

Finally the call came. "She's in labor. If you get down to the hospital, you'll have a chance to see your daughter as soon as she's born."

A lump filled Margaret's throat. They'd lost four babies, but they wouldn't lose this one. "God's so good. I knew it would all work out."

Bill nodded. "Isn't it amazing? Miraculous."

On the way to the hospital, the two of them went over the attorney's instructions. They could visit with the baby while she was in the hospital and as often as they wanted during the forty-eight-hour period when the birth mother could change her mind.

When Margaret and Bill entered the waiting room, their attorney was there, talking with a doctor and the social worker. Something was obviously wrong.

As their attorney led them into the hallway, Margaret's heart was pounding in her throat. He sighed hard. "The birth mother's wavering."

Margaret thought she was dreaming. They'd done everything they could to avoid this. "Wavering?"

Bill leaned against the wall. The impossible had happened, just the way he'd feared, and now he looked drained of all hope. "So it's a done deal?"

"Not entirely. Her first baby was a boy, and apparently she never wanted a boy. And when she found out this baby was a girl, she didn't believe it. Now, she's saying all her life she's wanted a daughter. But it might just be last-minute jitters."

Three hours later the terrible news they'd been dreading was confirmed. The birth mother was adamant and apologetic, but she wanted to keep her baby.

The couple left the hospital in a fog. Margaret wanted to pray but she couldn't. The loss was just as great as every miscarriage — a silent sort of grief and loss other people seldom understand.

For weeks after losing the baby girl, Margaret thought about the child. What sort of life would she have? The questions were so daunting, the loss so great, she had no interest in starting the process over again. She and Bill decided they would shelve the idea of parenting for now. If God didn't want them to raise a child, they couldn't do anything to force the issue.

But one day three months later, the social worker called. "I've got another baby girl. She was born a week ago and apparently the family she was headed for had already been given another child. So this baby girl is yours if you're interested. The mother waived her rights to the child. There is no danger of a change in plans."

Bill and Margaret looked at each other and their answer was immediate. "Yes."

Overnight, they were the parents of an angel baby, a child they named Brianna Suzanne. God had answered their prayer after all. But they didn't realize the true miracle until they took a call from the social worker six months later.

"I have some bad news. The child you lost out on had a rare heart condition. She died last week."

The news hit Margaret like a baseball bat in the stomach. She sat down, cradling her daughter close to her chest. "I'm sorry. Please . . . tell the mother we'll pray for her."

When the conversation was over, Margaret remembered her prayer. *Please, God . . . we can't lose another child.* She studied her daughter's small features and tried to imagine losing her now, after six months. God knew they could not handle that. And instead God brought them Brianna Suzanne, a miracle baby in more ways than they had known until that morning.

> As a father has compassion on his children, so the LORD has compassion on those who fear him; for he knows how we are formed, he remembers that we are dust.
>
> PSALM 103:13–14

WEEK 6.
MIRACLE OF THE HEART

SCRIPTURE READING:
GENESIS 29:31–35

Wait for the LORD; be strong and take heart and wait for the LORD.

PSALM 27:14

Kate English fell in love with Kurt after her junior year in college. He shared her faith and love of the outdoors and he wanted a whole houseful of kids. Kate felt that God had hand-delivered Kurt to her. Wedding plans were under way.

But a few months later, their car was hit head-on by a drunk driver. Kurt broke his leg, but Kate was left with a crushed pelvis, internal injuries, and a jagged scar across her right cheek. Because of the pelvic damage, she would never be able to have children.

Three weeks after the accident Kurt visited Kate and poured out his feelings. "I'm having second thoughts about getting married. I want children, Kate. The reason I want to get married is to have a family."

41

His words pierced her heart. "I can't have kids, so you don't want to marry me."

"I'm sorry. I know it sounds terrible, but I can't change the way I feel." It was the last time Kate ever saw him.

She spent two months in the hospital and then went home to complete her rehabilitation. Every day she fell deeper into a depression. She had lost her fiancé, her good looks, and her ability to have children. Even her faith, because she felt God allowed it to happen.

Finally, her parents insisted on counseling and over the course of the next year Kate began to find a new life, earning her Emergency Medical Technician certificate. Gradually her faith returned, and she found great peace in her relationship with God. No matter if Kurt had left, no matter how many people stared at her face, God would be there for her. He hadn't allowed the car accident. Drunk drivers were part of a fallen world. And she couldn't navigate a fallen world without God.

Kate pursued becoming a paramedic with a passion, and the job turned out to be everything she hoped it would be. But she always felt men were looking at her scar, not seeing who she was on the inside. And so she kept walls up around her heart. All the while two desires burned in her heart.

"Please, God, help me learn to love. Bring someone into my life who will accept me the way I am. And please let me care for a child one day."

Months became years and still Kate felt helpless to move beyond her fears. Finally, on the morning of her twenty-seventh birthday she prayed, "God, if you don't want me to find love, if children aren't in my future, so be it. I give my whole life over to you."

That day Kate and Tom, a single paramedic whom she'd known for three years, were dispatched to the scene of a fatality. The victims' car had gone off the freeway and rolled into a ravine. A deceased man and a woman were trapped inside the crushed car. Special machinery was working to get the bodies out, and halfway through the procedure the small, stifled cries of a child came from the backseat.

Kate and Tom rushed past the other workers. Strapped in the backseat were two children — an infant in a car seat, eyes wide open and alert. And a boy, maybe two or three years old, in an upright car seat. He was crying, his head bleeding, his eyes filled with terror.

In fifteen minutes Kate and Tom were able

to get the children out of the vehicle. Kate stayed with them, taking their vital signs, making sure they had no serious injuries. The boy held tight to Kate's hand and his little sister's hand and cuddled close to Kate. By the time Tom had helped to remove the bodies of the two adults, Kate felt a bond with the children that went beyond explanation.

Details came in. The children's mother was in jail and had signed over her parental rights to her only living relative — her sister. The deceased couple was the sister and her husband, both of whom were drunk. The boy's name was Peter, and his sister was Cassie. They were placed in a temporary foster home.

But Kate couldn't get the little boy out of her head. A week after the accident, Kate dreamed she was caring for little Peter and Cassie. Parenting them. The next morning she talked to Tom. "I'm thinking of seeing if I can get emergency approval to foster them, maybe even adopt them one day."

Tom's eyes sparkled. "Let me know if it works out. I'll do whatever I can to help."

Four weeks after the accident, Peter and Cassie were placed in her home as long-term foster kids. From the beginning Kate knew they were an answer to prayer in her life.

Tom came around several times a week. Sometimes he'd play with Peter or rock Cassie to sleep. Other times he'd stay and talk to Kate about his life and dreams. What started as a friendship soon became more. Tom told Kate he was falling in love with her, and Kate fought her desire to shut him out.

Six months later, Kate got approval to officially adopt the children. That night, Tom pulled out a ring and asked her the question she never expected to hear again. "Will you marry me, Kate? Let me love you all the days of my life?"

Tears filled her eyes as Kate took the ring, kissed Tom, and told him yes. They were married on her twenty-eighth birthday. Two months later, Kate and Tom stood hand in hand as a judge finalized the adoption, and Kate marveled at the turns her life had taken.

One car accident had shut the door on what she thought was her future, but the other had brought about not one, but two miracles.

. . . to bestow on them a crown of beauty
instead of ashes, the oil of gladness

45

instead of mourning, and a garment of praise instead of a spirit of despair.

ISAIAH 61:3

Week 7.
A Time to Go Home

SCRIPTURE READING:
LUKE 15:11–32

"I know the plans I have for you," declares the LORD, "plans to prosper you and not to harm you, plans to give you hope and a future."

JEREMIAH 29:11

Brian T. Noble was the son of loving parents in New Orleans, Louisiana, but as a teenager, he grew restless to experience the wilder side of life. Shortly after his sixteenth birthday, he decided to drop out of school.

"Brian, I absolutely will not hear of it." His mother shook her head, clearly disgusted by the idea.

"But Mom, I wanna be a prizefighter!"

"A fighter?" She raised her hand in his direction. "No son of mine is going to leave school for prizefighting. Besides, God has a good future for you. Good plans and a good life. Don't throw it all away."

But Brian's frustrations grew, and he put into action a plan to run away from home

47

after school was out for the summer. He was an intelligent young man, tall and athletic, with a strong sense of survival. He discovered that by watching the railroad cars, he could determine approximately where they were headed. He recognized the dangers of jumping onto a moving train but wasn't afraid. If his timing was right, he believed he could safely jump aboard a slow-moving cargo car.

Summoning his courage, Brian studied a train that appeared to be heading north. Perfect. He made his move, knowing that if he missed, he could fall under the wheels and be crushed to death. Jumping at the right moment, he landed safely inside the boxcar.

He used this new mode of transportation several times over the next few days until he reached a small Kansas town. There he saw what appeared to be a traveling circus. Hungry and out of money, Brian was hired to help set up and tear down the various rides. But his eyes lit up when he spotted a sign: "Fighters needed — go three rounds with a paying customer." The pay was more than Brian would make in a week.

Having found a place to stay and a way to make money, he sent a letter to his parents the next morning.

■ ■ ■ ■

In New Orleans, Brian's parents had been worried sick. They prayed constantly, begging God to give them a sign that their son was all right. They opened his letter together, tears gathering for both of them.

They read the words, "Dear Mom and Dad . . . I'm sorry for leaving without saying good-bye, but I knew you wouldn't let me go. I can't tell you where I am, but I'm safe . . . and I might do some prizefighting."

Over the next eight months, Brian traveled with the circus to dozens of towns and participated in the pit fights, in which two men went into a sunken pit and fought until one man dropped. Brian never lost a fight. He wrote his parents assuring them that he was living his dream and not to worry.

Meanwhile, Brian's parents could do nothing *but* worry about him. He was a drifter and a fighter. They prayed daily for God to keep him safe and bring him home soon.

In the cold of February, the crowds dwindled and his circus folded. Hearing that the nearest traveling circus was about twenty miles south, he knew just the train to take him there. But as he hid under the station's loading dock, waiting for the perfect moment to hop onboard, he noticed that two locomotives were being hooked to the train. That meant the train would pick up a great deal of speed quickly. It might even be traveling close to full speed as it left the station. *That's okay,* he told himself. He'd jumped fast trains before. He could do it again.

When the train moved, Brian ran toward a boxcar. But suddenly the ground beneath him narrowed, and he found himself sprinting alongside a steep ravine. He glanced ahead and saw that the tracks became a bridge. He had just one chance. If he missed, he would fall into a canyon to certain death.

Brian jumped. At first he grabbed hold of the boxcar floor, but the train picked up speed and he lost his grip. He started sliding out of the boxcar, gripping the edge with his fingertips. His body dangled dangerously over the edge and inch by inch his fingers slipped.

"No!" he shouted. "Please, God! Don't let me die!"

Suddenly, a tall black man appeared in what Brian had thought was the empty boxcar. The man stared at him intently. "It's time to go home, Brian." Then he reached down, grabbed Brian's hands, and pulled him into the speeding boxcar. Brian's sides heaved as he lay facedown on the floor to catch his breath.

He closed his eyes and uttered a silent prayer, still stunned that he was alive. Then he lifted his head to thank the man, but the boxcar was empty. He glanced outside and shuddered. There was no way the man could have jumped from the train and survived. He had simply disappeared.

Brian knew with great certainty that whoever the man was, his message had been right on. He stayed on the train until it reached New Orleans and returned home. After a tearful reunion, he told his parents about the man in the boxcar.

"An angel, son," his father said. "God is watching out for you. See, he brought you home to us."

Brian returned to school and a few months later was baptized. After graduating, he served in World War II with the Navy, taking part in twenty-eight combat missions in the South Pacific. After the war he returned to New Orleans, where he became a minister of one of the largest congregations in the city.

"God used that angel to not only save my life but to change it into something that would glorify him forever."

Before I formed you in the womb I knew you, before you were born I set you apart; I appointed you as a prophet to the nations.

JEREMIAH 1:5

WEEK 8.
THE MOST FRIENDS
OF ALL

SCRIPTURE READING:
DANIEL 1

Don't let anyone look down on you because you are young, but set an example for the believers in speech, in life, in love, in faith and in purity.

1 TIMOTHY 4:12

Larry Bradford was a social nobody at his high school. Yes, he was active in his church youth group, a high academic achiever, and an Eagle Scout. But his peers barely knew he was alive.

When his father would ask him about his friends, Larry would say, "The guys at school don't like me."

"Well, then that's what I'll pray for: that one day you'll have more friends than anyone in your class."

Larry thought his father was crazy to believe that was possible. Besides, his dad was all the friend he ever needed.

But when Larry was a junior his father suffered a fatal heart attack. Larry lost his closest friend — and then realized how few friends he had. He was not a part of any group at school. At lunch he sat by himself, reading his old leather Bible. Sometimes other kids called Larry a "Bible banger" or they'd ask, "How come you believe that stuff?"

"God's real. His truth is real," Larry would respond.

The hurtful comments didn't distract Larry. He was determined to become the devoted Christian man his father had been. When he graduated there were no emotions. He'd never connected with his classmates. He attended college and graduate school, married, and became a pediatrician. His wife gave him three daughters and a son, and Larry never regretted the past. He was very happy.

On Larry's thirty-seventh birthday he received two pieces of mail — the first inviting him to his high school twentieth reunion; the second confirming what his doctor had told him the day before: he had an aggressive lung cancer.

"We'll do everything we can medically," his doctor said. "But you better get people praying right away."

Larry drew his family together, and they began to pray and to ask everyone they knew to pray, too. He sent an e-mail to Robert Wills, the organizer of the class reunion, saying, "Robert, I've been diagnosed with lung cancer. I won't be attending the reunion. But please ask the class to pray. I'd appreciate it."

Robert received the e-mail and was cut to the heart. Larry Bradford? The good guy, the Bible reader? Stricken with lung cancer? Robert sent an e-mail to the entire class explaining why Larry wouldn't be attending. He included Larry's e-mail address.

That's when the miracle began to play out. One by one Larry began receiving e-mails.

From the football quarterback — a cocky, foulmouthed kid: "Larry, you were an inspiration to us all. This world needs you. I'll be praying."

From a pretentious guy in his algebra class: "Larry, remember how you read your Bible and the rest of us didn't get it? Well, I get it today. I'm a Christian now, and maybe it's all because you never backed down about your faith. You've got a friend here who'll be praying for you every day."

If Larry was to have any chance of survival, one of his lungs had to be removed. During his recovery in the hospital his wife brought him his laptop computer. Dozens of e-mails from former classmates filled the box.

"When my wife left me," one guy wrote, "I was so alone, I thought about ending it. But then I remembered you, sitting by yourself eating lunch and reading your Bible. You had no one and you were always so happy, man. I bought a Bible and found a church. I've been a believer ever since. Fight hard, friend. You have no idea the difference you've made in my life."

Against all odds, Larry began to improve. The reunion was two months away, and Robert Wills sent out another e-mail. "Pray he can come to the reunion. It's time we show Larry how many friends he has now." And so they continued to pray.

Three weeks before the reunion, Larry received great news. The surgery appeared to have removed all the cancer. Larry's radiation and chemotherapy sessions would be tapered off and possibly discontinued.

"I think you should go to the reunion," his wife said.

Larry wasn't sure. It would mean a flight and several days away. He took his wife's hand. "Go with me?"

Her smile still melted his heart. "Definitely."

The night of the big event, Robert Wills

saw Larry enter the hall first and others began smiling at him, standing, clapping. A chill ran down Larry's spine, and he stopped short. His wife leaned close. "I thought you said you weren't popular."

In less than a minute, everyone was on their feet, their applause filling the room. "Larry! Larry! Larry!"

Robert gave him a microphone. "Talk to 'em, Larry. Half of them only came to see you, to thank you for showing them what it means to have faith."

The night was amazing, full of conversations Larry was sure he'd remember as long as he lived. The people who had shown him no concern now felt a shared sense of faith. Most special for Larry were the people who pulled him aside and apologized.

"It's a miracle," his wife said later. "The doctors didn't think you'd live this long, and look at you."

Larry smiled. "I would've had my miracle even if I hadn't been well enough to come to the reunion. Twenty-three years ago my father prayed I'd have more friends than anyone in my class. Incredible."

Two years later, Larry died. The funeral service was a standing-room-only event, attended by his family, friends, colleagues, and neighbors. And more than a hundred of his high school classmates.

When he arrived and saw the evidence of the grace of God, he was glad and encouraged them all to remain true to the Lord with all their hearts.

ACTS 11:23

WEEK 9.
A VOICE IN THE STORM

SCRIPTURE READING:
PSALM 107

My flesh and my heart may fail, but God is the strength of my heart and my portion forever.

PSALM 73:26

Kody Watts laced his hiking boots, slipped on a parka, and set out for a winter hike. That morning he'd gotten into a fight with his parents over what he was going to do after graduation. They wanted him to go to college, but he thought college could wait. He was thinking of something daring and adventurous.

His mother had said, "Just listen to what God's telling you to do." But he wasn't so sure God talked to people, especially him.

His parents' home was within walking distance of a large lake that had a thick layer of ice over it, except for patches of thin ice in the middle. His plan was to hike around the lake's perimeter and think about his life. As he reached the frozen shore, he saw storm clouds gathering in the northwest.

As a boy, Kody wanted to become an emergency room doctor. But after his ninth-grade year, he struggled with science and math. Then there were football and basketball and, well, lots of girls. All of which left little time for studying. Kody pulled Cs and Bs, and that wouldn't get the university to even consider him.

Kody kept walking for nearly an hour about a hundred yards offshore. It was getting colder fast and the dark clouds had moved in over the lake. He wasn't quite halfway around the frozen lake when the snow began falling, so he turned around. He hadn't even left a note for his parents, so they had no idea where he was.

Okay, God, get me home safe. He'd been caught in storms before — just not this far from home. But he always felt closer to God when he was outdoors. The Lord would be right beside him as he walked.

Minutes later, the clouds darkened and seemed to almost settle on top of the ice. As Kody picked up his pace, the snow fell harder and he could no longer see the shore. He kept his gaze straight ahead, but all at once a fierce wind swept over him and he was in a complete whiteout.

Afraid he might be heading toward the

middle of the lake, Kody turned left, moving toward what he hoped was the shore. The blizzard was intensifying with each passing moment. After ten minutes, he figured he should have reached the shore. Ten more minutes went by, and a wave of panic pierced his heart. The temperature had dropped below zero and the air was burning his lips and throat, making his lungs ache.

Kody began jogging but hit a chunky section of ice and stumbled. Struggling to his feet, he realized he'd completely lost his sense of direction and couldn't even see his hands. A rush of dizziness swept over him and as he tried to move he fell again. He'd also lost his sense of balance. Then he realized he was snow-blind.

Kody tried to stand up and again fell to the ice. Yes, that was it. He'd read about it happening to people and knew it was deadly. He couldn't tell up from down because of the blinding snow. *God, I'm in big trouble. Please, help me!*

"Keep moving," he ordered himself. Reaching forward, he dug his fingers into the snow and pulled his body along. The dizziness made him feel sick to his stomach.

"Help me, God!" His cry was swallowed up in the wind.

At that moment, Kody heard the deep resonant sound of the foghorn, located at the rescue station at the edge of the lake, just blocks from his house. Then he heard a voice speaking over the station's public-address system. "Be careful. You're very close to broken ice at the middle of the lake. Stay to the right and climb the concrete wall when you reach it."

Kody opened his eyes, his heart racing with hope. The whiteout was as strong as ever, but somehow the man at the rescue station had seen him. Kody began slithering toward the voice inch by inch. Finally, he reached the wall. Peering through the storm, he saw the light ahead. He climbed over the retaining wall and felt his way through deep drifts of snow toward the door of the rescue station.

He saw the door open and could feel himself being pulled inside by a large bearded man, who helped him into a chair and offered him a mug of hot coffee.

"Thank you." Kody was too stunned to say anything else, though his heart was full. Instead, he stared at the man who saved his life. Who was the guy? Normally the rescue station was closed for the winter.

The man looked intently at Kody. His eyes were crystal blue, a color Kody had never seen before. "You were lost out there and close to the open water, so I sounded the foghorn."

"How could you see me?" Kody was still freezing.

"You asked for help. That's my job."

"Rescue worker, you mean?"

"You could say that. I needed to keep you safe."

"Why are you here, anyway?"

"Doing research." The man winked at him.

As they were speaking, the weather cleared. It had been seven hours since Kody left home, and he thought of his parents. "I better get going." He stood and shook the man's hand. "Thanks again. You saved my life."

His parents were about to call the police when Kody walked into the house. They were at his side immediately. It took Kody ten minutes to tell his story.

"That's impossible." His father's voice was gentle. "I went by the station the other day. It said, 'Closed for winter October to April.'"

Frustration welled up in Kody. "Listen, I can still taste the coffee. The guy saved my life."

Determined to find the man, Kody walked

back to the rescue building the next morning. The station was locked tightly, a chain through its double doors. The back door was nearly buried under a three-foot-high snowdrift. It showed no signs of having been disturbed in weeks.

Baffled, Kody remembered that the county sheriff's department ran the rescue station. He hurried home and called but was told no one had access to the rescue station. A call to the university told him that the county did not allow research at the station in the winter.

Kody hung up the phone and fell to his knees, weak with the realization that God had worked a miracle to save his life. And if God wanted his life saved, it must be so that he himself could go on to save the lives of others. And that meant going to college to study medicine. Just as he used to dream of doing when he was younger.

Today Kody is at medical school. And though he can't prove it, he's convinced that the man who saved his life was an angel. An angel sent to show him the way home . . . and the way to a future that God had planned for him all along.

Show me your ways, O LORD, teach me
your paths.

PSALM 25:4

WEEK 10.
BUCKLE UP

SCRIPTURE READING:
GENESIS 27

Listen to your father, who gave you life, and do not despise your mother when she is old.

PROVERBS 23:22

Andy Conner headed for the front door just as his mother came down the stairs. Andy and his best friend, Jared, were interns for the Birmingham, Alabama, firehouse, and Jared was outside in his car waiting.

"Fire drills again?" His mother smiled at him.

"Yep. See you around midnight."

"Be safe." It was something she said often, especially since Andy's father had died a year earlier.

"I'm always safe. That's my job, Mom, remember?"

She muttered, "Because of Jared."

Andy stared at her. "What?" His tone grew harsh. "I'm not in this because of Jared. I'm in it for me."

"Be real. Since third grade if Jared did it, you did."

Andy had turned nineteen that fall, and his mother's words grated on him. "I'm my own person, Mom."

He turned and walked out. He understood that she worried about him. But couldn't she see how much he enjoyed working for the fire department?

Andy climbed into Jared's car and they sped off toward the station. It was fourteen miles away on a winding two-lane road.

Jared turned to Andy. "Bad day?"

"My mom's trying everything to change my mind about firefighting." Did she really believe that he'd done everything Jared had ever done?

Andy had prayed more since his father's death. Talking with God made him feel as if he had a dad to talk to again, and now, Andy did just that. *God, help me be my own man.*

Usually when he prayed, he sensed that God was right there whispering an answer. But with his angry heart, he felt nothing.

From her living room Beth Conner watched Jared's car drive away. Why did Andy have to get so mad? She hated that he wanted to be a firefighter. The thought of Andy in a burning building paralyzed her with fear.

Andy had never mentioned firefighting until Jared got interested in it. Since the boys met in grade school, Andy had been Jared's tag-along pal, which hadn't always been good. There were many times when following Jared got Andy into trouble. *If only I'd broken up their friendship years ago, Andy wouldn't be pursuing such a dangerous job.*

The reason the boys had stayed close was because of her husband, Joe. His attitude about Jared had always been positive. But she was convinced that Jared was leading Andy into places she didn't want him to go.

She exhaled hard. What was this feeling strangling her heart? For a moment she considered her frustration and suspicion and, yes, meanness she exuded so often. Then her eyes shifted to the Bible sitting on the table. *God, I need your help.*

For a long while she waited, and then slowly a feeling began to surface in her heart. First, she needed to give Andy back to God. "I can't keep him safe, God. So you take care of him."

Second, she needed to believe that Jared was loyal to Andy. "Okay, God. Help me love Jared. Help me see Jared's friendship as a good thing."

The boys were halfway to the fire department when Jared turned to Andy. "You must really be mad at her."

"I guess. She said some rotten things."

"Wanna talk about it?"

"No." He would never let Jared know his mother didn't think him a good friend.

"Hey, put your belt on. Remember the rule?"

Andy remembered. *Firefighters show the way; buckle up every day.* Not that it mattered, right? Andy hesitated. He was about to do exactly what his mother had accused him of. "I don't like seat belts."

"You know something, Andy? All my life I've been lucky to be your friend."

"What's that supposed to mean?"

"I've been lucky to always have you." He glanced at Andy's seat belt. "So buckle it, okay? I need you."

Andy thought for a moment. Jared had never been so insistent. And it didn't make him a mindless follower if he buckled his seat belt, did it?

"Fine." He snapped the buckle into place.

At the same instant, Jared screamed, "Look out!"

A flash of something metallic filled the windshield and then the sound of screeching tires, shattering glass, and twisting metal. Dust filled the compartment and broken glass covered his legs, but Andy was alive. He glanced at Jared and saw that his friend looked unhurt.

"Can you believe that?" Jared was breathless.

A truck had swerved into Jared's lane, causing him to jerk the steering wheel. The car had careened off the roadway straight into a tree. Without the seat belt, Andy would have gone straight through the windshield.

Jared's advice was a miracle that saved his life.

Beth got the call an hour later. Andy explained how Jared had insisted he use his seat belt.

"I thought how you said that I have to do everything Jared says. I almost didn't use it because of that. But then Jared told me he needed me as a friend, and that's when I decided to buckle up."

Beth's hands began to tremble at the news. Her criticism of Jared had almost resulted in Andy's death. God had worked a miracle. And both of her prayers had been answered in an instant.

Beth couldn't wait to take Jared in her arms and thank him.

Do not embitter your children, or they will become discouraged.

COLOSSIANS 3:21

Week 11.
Letting Go

Do not be anxious about anything, but in everything, by prayer and petition, with thanksgiving, present your requests to God. And the peace of God, which transcends all understanding, will guard your hearts and your minds in Christ Jesus.

PHILIPPIANS 4:6–7

Kari Clausen was a woman who clung to the people she loved, especially to her children. She was overprotective, and there were nights when she couldn't sleep for fear they might get hurt. It was something she despised about herself, but it remained all the same.

"Help me have a looser hold on them, God," she would pray for Cole, five, and Anna, three. But inevitably she took to worrying again.

On the morning when the tragedy struck, Kari and her husband, Mel, were packing and loading their belongings into a trailer for a move from West Hills, California, to nearby Thousand Oaks. A loud crash from the backyard suddenly rang through the house.

"Cole! Anna!" Kari screamed as she raced out the back door. What she saw made her heart stand still. The three-hundred-pound steel ramp at the back of the trailer had come down onto the ground, and underneath it was Cole's limp body. Blood was oozing from his nose, mouth, and ears, and the ramp was resting on his head.

"Mel!" Kari screamed. "Help!"

Her husband was immediately at her side, and together they summoned a strength that was beyond their own, lifting the ramp off Cole's head. Blood began pouring from his sunken skull.

"My God, he's dead!" Kari was hysterical as Mel took the boy into his arms. "What do we do?"

With Mel's calming instructions, they were quickly in the car, racing toward Union Memorial Hospital.

"He's gonna die, Mel. I can't drive fast enough." Kari's hands shook and her heart raced.

"He's still breathing." Mel's voice was loud and insistent. "He's not going to die. You need to pray!"

Kari prayed for several moments, begging God to spare Cole's life. She began to sing the words of her favorite hymn, "Great is thy faithfulness . . . O God my Father," and a calm came over her heart.

She continued to drive as a realization hit her: she could do nothing to help Cole. He was completely in God's hands. The truth of that calmed her further.

"Pray for a miracle, Kari," Mel said quietly. "He's breathing slower."

"I am." Kari swallowed back a torrent of sobs. "God's in control." Then she recalled that Cole had asked Jesus to come and live in his heart, and peace came to her that his place in heaven was secure.

Pulling up to the hospital's emergency room entrance, Mel rushed the blood-covered child into an examination room. As they laid him on a table, Cole began to cough and cry. "I'm choking."

Kari felt sick as she realized he was choking on his own blood. She took hold of his hand as once more his body went limp and his eyes closed.

Hearing what happened, a doctor said that Cole must be transferred to a hospital across town, where they had more sophisticated equipment for severe head injuries.

As they waited for the ambulance, two

nurses struggled to locate Cole's pulse. "We're losing him!" one of them shouted. "Get the doctor."

As Kari stepped back to get out of the way, Cole suddenly moved. In a surreal manner, his small shoulders rose so that he was nearly sitting straight up. It seemed as if someone was supporting him with invisible hands behind his back. His long, black eyelashes fluttered and his eyes opened, staring blankly.

In a weak voice he said, "Jesus, please take care of me." Then his eyes shut and he sank back down.

The nurses looked at each other in disbelief and then at the Clausens, who were also stunned by what had happened. Before a word could be spoken, the ambulance attendants rushed in and whisked the boy away.

Early tests showed that Cole had suffered extensive damage, shattering his skull and sending bone fragments into the area of the brain that controls speech, hearing, and memory. The neurosurgeon explained that it required immediate surgery and warned that *if* Cole survived, he would not be the same boy he had been.

For six hours Kari and Mel and family prayed as the surgeons worked. Again, Kari felt an overwhelming sense of peace. God was in control . . . even of her fears.

Finally, the doctor came in and motioned for them to follow. "Come say hello to Cole," he said.

Kari gasped softly. "He's . . . he's . . ."

The doctor smiled. "Come see for yourself."

They followed the doctor to Cole's bedside. His head was swathed in bandages. As Kari reached out her fingers toward him, a tiny burp escaped his mouth.

"Excuse me," he whispered.

Kari felt a surge of elation. He could speak! They had not lost Cole after all. Happy tears flowed.

Despite obvious signs of success, doctors continued to warn the Clausens that Cole could take a turn for the worse — bleeding, blood clots, seizures. Worst of all, he carried a significant risk of developing a brain infection.

Cole had to undergo a series of painful intravenous antibiotic treatments to counteract the risk of what could be a fatal complication. During the first night, he moaned from nausea and said, "Mommy, pray for me."

In that instant, Kari felt her heart soar. If Cole could see clearly enough that the solution was prayer, she had no doubts he would survive. She prayed as she'd never truly prayed before . . . with confidence.

Through the next three days, whenever Cole was awake, he asked for only one thing — "Pray for me."

The following day, Cole was moved to intensive care, where he got up and walked to the bathroom by himself, talked nonstop, and played with Legos.

The technician who did Cole's initial CAT scan stopped by and told Kari, "I never in a million years thought he'd live or ever be like this again, especially not so soon. I've never seen anything like it."

The intravenous treatments were harrowing. The strong medication burned throughout Cole's body for the entire thirty-minute treatment. During the last treatment, Kari prayed that Cole would feel no pain, and remarkably he never so much as stirred or cried out.

It was the second time since Cole's injury that God had clearly proven he was in control. After ten days in the hospital, they were able to bring Cole home. Time passed, and Cole healed completely.

For a time, Cole didn't remember anything about what happened, but one day he told Kari that he had pulled the pin and made the trailer ramp fall.

"It really hurt," he said. "But then Jesus came. He was just . . . all white. Then you and Daddy came and lifted the ramp off my head."

Kari shuddered. "Is that all you remember?"

"Jesus came to see me when we got to the hospital, too. He lifted me up and I asked him to help me. Then he hugged me and said, 'Cole, you're going to be okay.' "

Kari's mind flew back to that moment and tears flowed. Taking him in her arms, she could sense another set of arms enfolding both of them, arms that had been there when there was nothing more she could do for him.

Did I not tell you that if you believed, you would see the glory of God?

JOHN 11:40

Week 12.
When Life Changed in an Instant

SCRIPTURE READING:
PSALM 116

In my distress I called to the LORD; I called out to my God. From his temple he heard my voice; my cry came to his ears.

2 SAMUEL 22:7

Rain poured from the skies that day, but Michelle Conley's future couldn't have been brighter. She was an intelligent, pretty high school senior with dozens of friends and a fiancé named Bobby Barrows. They planned to marry after he graduated from college.

Michelle's drive to work had been uneventful until her Honda began to shake from a sudden force of wind. She began to brake, then . . . everything went black.

A minute earlier, Jonas Green stepped out of his auto body shop and was shocked to see a tornado dropping out of the sky directly onto a blue Honda on the roadway before him. The car flipped three times, slammed into a ditch, and was lifted once more before slamming down in an adjacent field. Jonas called 911, then ran toward the car.

Inside the car, Michelle opened her eyes. What had happened? Suddenly she realized her body lay partway out the empty back frame. Her head rested on the car's twisted trunk, while the rest of her body lay at an awkward angle along the backseat. Her left leg was crushed between the front seat and the door. When she tried to move, a searing pain burned in her back and her body remained motionless.

"Dear God, help me!"

At that instant Jonas reached the car. "Don't move, honey. My name's Jonas and the ambulance is coming. Tell me your phone number and I'll call your parents."

Michelle moaned, then choked out the number.

Jonas disappeared with the information. Suddenly two more men ran up to the car. One of them leaned in and said, "You're gonna be fine, Michelle. Just lie still."

"What happened?" Michelle's teeth were chattering.

The other man said, "A tornado destroyed your car. But you're going to be okay. Just keep believing that."

At that moment, the voices of the men faded away. When she came to, paramedics were working to free her from the wreckage and she could hear her father's voice.

Michelle opened her eyes. "Daddy, look at my car."

"Don't worry about it. Let's take care of you."

"Where's the other two guys?" she asked Jonas.

"I'm the only one who's been here except for the paramedics."

Michelle closed her eyes as the paramedics fitted a brace around her neck. She heard them discussing her back injury. *No, God! Please don't let my back be broken.* Everything began to fade again. She recalled the two men. *You'll be okay. Believe that.* How strange that Jonas hadn't seen them. How had they known her name?

When Michelle awoke, she was in a hospital bed. Screws protruded from her temples and weights dangled from her skull. She was strapped to a device that seemed to stretch her body, but she could feel none of it.

At that moment, a doctor entered the room.

"Hi," she whispered. "I'm going to be okay, right?"

The doctor moved closer to her. "Michelle, you crashed headfirst into the rear windshield, breaking your back and crushing your spinal cord. You're paralyzed from the neck down. You will not walk again."

Michelle wanted to scream. Her mind racing, she thought of the words of the two men. Then her parents came into the room, tears streaming down their faces.

"It's not true," she said. "I've asked God to heal me, and he will. I will walk again. I will graduate with my class. And I'm going to marry Bobby."

Her father said, "If anyone can do it, you can."

"We're all praying," her mother said. "And we'll keep praying until you can walk again."

Outside in the hallway, Bobby Barrows was in a state of shock. His mind was racked with despair as he considered their plans for the future. He and Michelle shared a strong faith, but it was hard to see God's plan.

Bobby entered her room and saw the tears trickle onto her cheeks. He took her limp hand in his. "I love you," he said, then kissed her tenderly on the lips. "We'll make it through this together, Michelle. We can't ever stop believing."

For three days Michelle tried desperately to move her fingers and toes, with no success. Then the doctor decreased the weight on her head, and suddenly she was able to move her right leg and both arms. The doctor's eyes grew wide in amazement, and he summoned another doctor into the room. When she moved again, he said, "That's impossible."

Michelle smiled. "I'll walk again; wait and see."

Later that week Michelle's mother read the amazing words of hope and promise in Psalm 116 to her. Michelle clung to the words, *"That I may walk before the LORD in the land of the living."*

Two months passed, and doctors performed surgery on Michelle's neck, placing her in a halo brace to help stabilize her broken back. She continued to amaze the doctors by regaining strength and movement. They said, "It's a miracle. We have no other explanation."

Less than three months after the accident, Michelle was released from the hospital. A week later, using a cane, she received a standing ovation as she hobbled to the podium to accept her high school diploma.

One year later, Michelle walked gracefully down a church aisle and married her childhood sweetheart.

"Do you think the men were angels?" Bobby asked.

Michelle smiled. "How else can you explain them?"

Indeed. Two years later, again defying medical understanding, Michelle gave birth to the couple's first child. Today she and Bobby have three children.

"Never limit God," Michelle tells her children. "I'm living proof that he hears us and he does answer."

With man this is impossible, but with God all things are possible.

MATTHEW 19:26

Week 13.
The Gift of Dance

SCRIPTURE READING:
2 SAMUEL 9

You will go out in joy and be led forth in peace; the mountains and hills will burst into song before you, and all the trees of the field will clap their hands.

ISAIAH 55:12

Isabelle Sims had never felt more discouraged. She was twenty-five years old with a noticeable weakness on her left side, the effects of being born with cerebral palsy. And that afternoon she had attempted the impossible, joining more than seventy applicants for the position of dance instructor at a prestigious New York arts school.

Part of the interview included a solo dance routine. Isabelle had the credentials and experience but there was no way her dance held up to those of the other young women. She left the building in tears and made the hour-long ride to her mother's house. Isabelle thought of how being a dance instructor had been the single dream she'd nurtured since she was a young girl — helping other children find the wings to fly across the stage the way she would have done if not for her handicap.

The moment her mother answered the door, tears filled Isabelle's eyes and she fell into her mother's arms.

"Honey, what happened?" Isabelle's mother, Lucy, held her tight, finally helping her inside where they sat in the living room side by side.

"They'll never hire me." Isabelle covered her face with her hands. "The other applicants were graceful and smooth. Who wants a dance instructor who limps?"

Without saying a word Lucy stood and slipped a tape into the VCR. When she returned to her spot next to Isabelle, she hit the Play button. The screen came alive with the image of Isabelle as a beautiful nine-year-old, twirling and leaping in the air at her first dance recital. Isabelle stared and wondered how she'd lost touch with that young girl. "I had so much confidence back then."

Her mother stopped the film and reached for Isabelle's hand. "You were such a little fighter, sweetheart. Nothing was going to stop you."

Isabelle sniffed. "That was a long time

ago. That little girl doesn't exist anymore."

Lucy drew a slow breath. "Darling, I think you need to hear the miracle story one more time."

Isabelle shrugged. She'd heard the story of her birth a dozen times, and it always brought hope. "Tell me."

"It was 1984," Lucy began. "Having had two miscarriages, I prayed daily that you would survive the pregnancy. I wanted you so badly, Isabelle."

One morning, though, when she was twenty-four weeks pregnant, she started having regular contractions. "The doctor told me you couldn't survive if you were born then. While the nurses set up an IV with drugs to try to stop the contractions, your father and I prayed for a miracle. I knew in my heart you were going to live."

When the medication took effect, Isabelle's father had fallen asleep. "Suddenly I couldn't draw a breath or make a sound. Finally I found the nurse's button. While I waited for help, I pinched off the intravenous line to the medication. About that time your father woke up and shouted for help. Nurses came immediately and realized I was having a rare side effect to the medication."

In ten minutes the danger had passed for Isabelle's mother. But not for Isabelle.

"Without the medication, my labor pains grew worse. An hour later they flew me to Chicago where the hospital would be better equipped to deal with that type of extreme premature birth."

Two days later, despite the doctor's efforts, Isabelle was born by C-section. "I was awake the whole time. I wanted to see you, even if only for a few minutes."

Twenty minutes after the surgery began, Isabelle was born. Fourteen inches long and just over a pound, she wiggled furiously, trying to draw her first breath. "The doctor took one look at you and said, 'She's a fighter.' It was almost like watching a miracle."

Isabelle's heart swelled with love as she pictured her mother, staring at her in those early moments.

"The doctors immediately sent you to the neonatal intensive care unit and put you on a ventilator inside a sterile, covered bassinet." Three days later, Isabelle was still gaining ground. For the next three months, she grew in the hospital. "You would kick at the wires and tubing around you. 'Keep fighting, Isabelle.' I told you that every day we were together. "It was truly amazing to see you grow a little stronger each day."

Finally, after four weeks, Lucy got to hold

her daughter for the first time. "It was the most emotional five minutes of my life. To have you in my arms, where you belonged. You were working so hard, too, to fight off infections and life-threatening illnesses."

When Isabelle's weight had climbed to five pounds, the doctors gave her permission to go home. "The doctors told us the risks were far from over. Cerebral palsy was the primary concern. When a baby is premature, even a slight jarring motion can cause the brain to bleed, causing cerebral palsy."

In Isabelle's case, a sonogram had detected a low-grade bleed during her time in the hospital. Once she was home, a physical therapist monitored her condition weekly. The months passed and became years. When Isabelle was a toddler, it became obvious that she struggled with her gross motor skills.

"The doctors told us that though it was a miracle you were alive, you had cerebral palsy on your left side. They said you would never learn to walk. We decided that only God could determine that."

As Isabelle grew, she encountered numerous challenges, but she fought hard to overcome every obstacle. "You learned to walk by the time you were three and when you turned six, you began to dance."

At that point in the story Lucy hit the Play button on the remote control. Isabelle could hardly see the dancing girl through the tears in her eyes. *I wasn't supposed to walk. Yet there I was, dancing. And no one in the world could have made me stop.*

When the segment ended, Lucy leaned over and hugged Isabelle close. Then she tenderly touched a single finger to the area over her daughter's heart. "The fighter is still in there, honey. No matter what happens, keep fighting. Because all of life is a dance."

Isabelle clung to her mother's words while she waited for word about the position. No longer was she discouraged by her limitations. Rather, she was reminded that every day, every breath, every step in the dance was a reason to celebrate.

And that attitude made it all the better two weeks later when she received a phone call from the art school. "Isabelle, we'd be honored if you'd accept our offer. We think you'll make an outstanding dance instructor."

It was the very best dream come true. Isabelle imagined how her mother would take the news, the way it would prove her right again that Isabelle was a living miracle. In that moment, Isabelle knew without a doubt that her mother was right about something else, too. The music still played; indeed, it would always play.

And never again would Isabelle stop dancing.

Timothy, my son, I give you this instruction in keeping with the prophecies once made about you, so that by following them you may fight the good fight.

1 TIMOTHY 1:18

WEEK 14.
HUMBLE YOURSELF

SCRIPTURE READING:
PHILIPPIANS 2:1–18

Humble yourselves, therefore, under God's mighty hand, that he may lift you up in due time.

1 PETER 5:6

When her mother suggested she join an eight-member Christian singing group called Alive, Ashley Payton declared there was no way she'd go to Wyoming. She was a nineteen-year-old minister's daughter who had grown up in Southern California. The plan was that if a trial week of performing in Wyoming went well, she could travel with the group across the country, visiting churches for one year.

"Think about your dream," her mother said.

Ashley was blonde with brown eyes and her voice easily rivaled many professional recording artists'. She had dazzled audiences since she was four years old and pictured herself singing for thousands of people every night. After a few days, the possibilities loomed larger than her concerns about the small towns.

"I'll do it," she said. "Maybe this is my big break."

Her mother wrinkled her nose. "This trip isn't about getting discovered, Ashley. It's about serving God with your gift of music."

Ashley knew her mother was right, but privately she was certain this trip would break her music career open. She flew to Wyoming and met the rest of the singing group. Fred and Rita were the couple in charge, and they treated her like a daughter. After singing as lead vocalist at a different church every night that week, Ashley was hooked. And once the group set out on its national tour they would be in big cities with large audiences.

They traveled from one city to the next in Fred and Rita's motor home. Each night they would collect small donations that paid their expenses. At first, Ashley was thrilled to be singing with a professional group and watching people come to know God. But as time passed, the joy wore thin. She started to focus on the inconvenience of sharing a motor home with seven others and the times when the group's funds ran so low they could only afford fast food.

One afternoon, they stopped at a small town restaurant for a sit-down dinner. They noticed a man dressed in tattered rags just outside the front door. His weathered face and matted hair were covered with a layer of silt and dirt.

"Bum!" Ashley whispered to herself.

When Fred stopped and started a conversation with "Gus," Ashley was horrified, especially when she smelled the man's body odor and the alcohol on his breath. Ashley wanted to cover her face with a bag.

"I can't give you any money," Fred said. "But you could be our guest."

The grizzly old guy's eyes fell on Ashley. "Okay."

Once inside, the manager showed them to a table near the back of a large private room. Ashley sat down first and Fred motioned for Gus to sit next to her.

Great. Some life-changing music tour this turned out to be, huh, God? I should've just stayed home.

A putrid aroma surrounded Ashley like a cloud. For a moment she felt sorry for Gus, but then she thought it was his own fault. Too much drinking or drugs.

"So you say you're Christians, huh?" Gus asked. "Well, I have a few questions for you. If God loves me, why doesn't he get me off the streets?"

As Fred and others in the group began to tell Gus about how Jesus had died for him, Ashley realized she had never met anyone who understood so little about God. She forgot his dirty condition and listened closely.

"Jesus freed us from our sins," Fred was saying.

"Free? I've always been free."

"Not really," Ashley cut in on Gus. "When we're free in Christ, our circumstances don't really matter anymore. All that matters is that he's with us, he loves us, and he'll see us safely home in the end."

The moment Ashley finished speaking she felt guilty. She'd been complaining for weeks about her situation. Instead of using her gift of song to touch hearts for God, the tour had become all about her. Tears stung her eyes. *Forgive me, God, for judging people like Gus. Thinking I'm better. I'm so sorry.*

For the next half hour the group members took turns sharing why they had come to faith, and the certainty that God heard their prayers and worked miracles.

"Miracles, huh?" There was a sudden twinkle in Gus's eyes. "I believe in miracles, too."

After the meal, Fred offered Gus a ride to

the next town where he knew of a church that could help Gus. The man agreed but headed to the restroom in the back of the room. The others got up and agreed to meet Fred and Gus out front of the restaurant.

After the group had waited a long time, Fred came out the front door. "Did Gus come out this way?"

"No," Rita said. "Did you check the other exits?"

"I checked the bathroom. There's one emergency exit back behind the cook's station, but I would have seen him and the kitchen personnel saw no customer back there. This is the only way he could have come. It doesn't make sense. It's like he just disappeared."

The group scanned the streets, but Gus was gone.

Suddenly, a heart-stopping possibility washed over Ashley. "You don't think, maybe . . . he was an angel? It's possible, isn't it?"

Fred gazed at Ashley. "I guess we'll never know."

But Ashley was convinced that God had sent Gus to remind her of her purpose — not just while traveling with Alive, but her purpose in life. In fact, the trip wound up being life-changing, just as Ashley had hoped.

But not in the way she had expected.

Whoever exalts himself will be humbled, and whoever humbles himself will be exalted.

MATTHEW 23:12

WEEK 15.
ONE EASTER SUNDAY

SCRIPTURE READING:
JONAH 1–2

If the LORD had not been on our side . . .
the flood would have engulfed us, the torrent would have swept over us, the raging
waters would have swept us away.

PSALM 124:1–5

It was a beautiful Easter Sunday and Lola
Randall was full of thanks. Most people
were still trapped in the throes of the Great
Depression, but Lola's husband, Jeffrey, had
a job in Phoenix and his income provided a
small home and plenty of food for their
young family.

As they arrived at the home of Jeffrey's
parents and settled into the family room,
Lola glanced around to where two-and-a-
half-year-old Bonnie was playing with building blocks. Lola and Jeffrey had not been
able to afford a home when they first married, so this had been the child's first home
and she was still comfortable in it. Bonnie

had golden-red hair, green eyes, and fair skin.

Most of Lola's memories of the house were happy ones. But one memory always sent chills down her spine. When Bonnie was just three weeks old, a curtain rod had accidentally slipped and shot down into Bonnie's crib, grazing the unformed soft area of her skull.

The doctor had examined the injury and shook his head. "If it had hit a fraction of an inch in either direction, it would have pierced her head and she'd be dead. But she's fine. The good Lord must be looking out for your little one."

That Easter Sunday, the family eventually wandered into the front yard to enjoy the last bit of afternoon sunshine. The senior Randalls' backyard contained a man-made fishpond that was five feet by eight feet in diameter and four feet deep. A flagstone walkway surrounded the pond, which had rounded, sloping edges and contained several brightly colored goldfish. Bonnie loved the pond but she was not allowed to play in the backyard around it. There was no way for a child Bonnie's age to climb out of the pond if she fell in.

The adults had been in the front yard briefly when Lola scanned the yard.

"Where's Bonnie?" she asked. At that moment there was a shrill scream from the backyard. Racing toward the sound, Lola tore around the house with the others close behind her.

"Bonnie!" Lola screamed. The child was standing in the middle of the stone walkway, dripping wet and crying hysterically. "Oh, dear God," Lola said as she pulled her little daughter close.

Jeffrey stood nearby, gazing down at the stone walkway. "Look. The sidewalk is dry. I can't believe it."

The walkway was completely dry except for small pools of water that had collected underneath Bonnie. There were no footprints or drips of water leading from the pond to where Bonnie now stood.

Lola's eyes narrowed as she studied the walkway that circled the pond. "Do you think the sun dried it up?"

"No. Bonnie just got out of the water. And she could never climb out by herself. Whatever just happened was some kind of miracle. Remember how the doctor said God is looking out for our little Bonnie?"

Lola nodded. "It's true."

Throughout the evening, the Randalls tried to get their daughter to discuss the incident. But Bonnie would only cry fiercely.

Over time the couple gave up. Years passed and Bonnie grew. She had no memory of the incident but she carried a desperate fear of water. Eventually she married and moved onto the U.S. Army base where her husband was stationed. During that time she decided she had to do something about her fear, so she asked the chaplain if he could help her.

The chaplain gazed thoughtfully at the young woman now seated across from him. "Did you ever have an accident involving water?"

Bonnie thought back. "Yes. I was nearly three years old and my parents say I fell into my grandparents' fishpond. I don't remember it."

"Bonnie," he said, "if you can remember what happened, we might understand your fear."

Over a series of counseling appointments, the chaplain helped Bonnie to eventually recall the scene.

"I was in the backyard," she said, her eyes glazed over in concentration. "I can see a fishpond and I walked toward it. Inside were the biggest goldfish I'd ever seen. I wasn't supposed to touch them. But I wanted so badly to pet them just once. So I leaned over and suddenly I fell into the water." Bonnie screamed and covered her eyes. "I couldn't get out. I was thrashing about and swallowing water. My head was submerged and I was drowning." Suddenly Bonnie gasped. "That's what happened! I remember everything now."

The chaplain leaned forward in his chair. "Go on, Bonnie. What happened then?"

"I was sinking. Then suddenly there was a man above me dressed all in white. He reached into the water and lifted me up and set me down on the walkway."

"Where did he go then?" the chaplain asked.

Bonnie paused a moment, searching the long-ago scene that was unfolding before her eyes. "He just set me down and disappeared." Bonnie's eyes came back into focus. "That's impossible, isn't it, Pastor?"

"What do your parents say about the event?"

"Well, they say there were no wet footprints or water drips leading from the pond to where I was standing when they found me. The only water was beneath me. But how could the man in white get me there without a trace of water? You don't think . . . ?"

The chaplain smiled kindly. "I can't explain it fully, Bonnie, but in my opinion God saved your life. And a certain guardian angel may have returned to heaven with wings wet from the water of a goldfish pond."

"Because he loves me," says the LORD, "I will rescue him; I will protect him, for he acknowledges my name."

PSALM 91:14

WEEK 16.
A GIFT OF GOD

SCRIPTURE READING:
1 SAMUEL 1

I will send down showers in season; there will be showers of blessing.
EZEKIEL 34:26

Jared Winters fell for Allison Hayes the moment he saw her late one August afternoon before his freshman year. Allison was walking around the high school track. He was practicing with the football team when his eyes met hers and for a moment it seemed they were the only two on the field. She was tall with pale blonde hair and brown eyes — the most beautiful girl he'd ever seen.

School started two weeks later and Jared uttered one prayer — *Please, God, let me see her.* The answer came when Allison walked into his American history class. When the bell rang and Jared walked past her, she said, "Hi. Freshman football, right?"

Jared could barely feel his feet against the floor. She knew who he was! The two struck up a conversation and eventually through phone calls and study sessions, they grew close. Allison was the girl of Jared's dreams, and the truth became truer all the time. Their relationship carried over from high school to college.

Both Jared and Allison had been active in church youth groups through high school, and they never let their relationship get more physical than kissing. But the temptations were stronger at college, so they had made a covenant: "God, we promise to stay pure for you. Help us keep our promise. And please bless our relationship."

The blessings seemed to pour out and the summer before their junior year they got engaged and wedding plans were set in motion. Two months before their wedding, Jared purchased a condo, where they'd live.

"How many kids do you want?" Jared asked.

Allison shrugged. "Two at least, don't you think?"

"However many it takes to get a girl who looks like you — blonde hair and brown eyes."

After the wedding reception, Jared's mother whispered in Allison's ear: "Now you can give me those grandbabies I've been wanting!"

"Give us a while," Allison responded. "We haven't had our honeymoon yet."

But the truth was, she and Jared both wanted children sooner rather than later. On their one-year anniversary, they put away the birth control. One year passed, then two, but no babies. They discovered that Allison had trouble ovulating, and most of her eggs were not fully developed. For an entire year Allison tried fertility drugs, but nothing worked, and they finally gave up.

After grieving their loss and praying more about it, they concluded it was time to look into adoption. They met with an adoption agency counselor and agreed to adopt a child from Russia. When it came time to specify what sort of child they wanted to adopt, Jared privately told Allison, "I want to ask for a blonde, brown-eyed girl. But God has a perfect child, just for us, and I don't want to limit him."

Allison loved the fact that he was willing to give up on his long-held dream and leave it in God's hands. And so they filled out the forms with open-ended answers — any child, any sex, any hair color.

Six months later the adoption agency worker told them that a baby boy was available — six months old, brown hair, brown eyes, with a slightly misshapen foot. She explained that most of the babies from that region of Russia had dark hair and eyes. "Is the fact that he might have health issues going to be a problem for you?"

They had prayed about this child, refusing to limit God as to which type of baby he placed in their arms. Jared answered, "If that's the baby you found for us, then that's our son."

Eight weeks later, the couple boarded a plane for Russia. The next day they showed up for their appointment at the Russian orphanage.

"We are excited that you will adopt little Ina." The woman smiled.

Allison frowned. "I'm afraid there must be a mix-up." She set the boy's photograph on the desk between them. "This is the baby we're here to adopt."

The woman shook her head. "Ramon was a very sick baby. He was placed with a local couple who take sick children."

Jared's heart beat hard beneath his shirt. "But all along, we were told he was our baby. Now you're saying you have a little girl for us?"

"Yes." The orphanage worker smiled. "Ina is six months old, a beautiful little girl."

She would have dark hair and eyes, the same as the other orphanage children. But

Allison was afraid to ask the next question: "What physical issues does Ina have?"

"Ina's parents died in an accident. From everything we know, Ina is in perfect health."

Allison's head was spinning. Beside her, Jared squeezed her hand and Allison saw the determination in his eyes. Whatever baby God had planned for them would be theirs.

"Well, then, could we meet her?"

When the woman returned, she passed a baby bundled in a faded pink blanket into Jared's outstretched arms. As soon as they could see her face, Jared whispered, "She's beautiful."

Allison pulled the blanket down. Their new little daughter was perfect, but it was more than that. Ina had pale blonde hair and brown eyes.

"She looks . . ." Jared turned and stared at Allison. "She looks just like you."

Jared and Allison were delighted with Ina. A week later they went home and started their life together. But the biggest surprise came that fall when Allison found out she was pregnant. In fact, Allison and Jared went on to have four healthy, dark-haired little boys. Only Ina has Allison's blonde hair and brown eyes — a child who came as a gift of God and a reminder that dreams matter.

Thanks be to God for his indescribable gift!
2 CORINTHIANS 9:15

WEEK 17.
MIRACLE OF LOVE

SCRIPTURE READING:
1 CORINTHIANS 13

Let the little children come to me, and do not hinder them, for the kingdom of heaven belongs to such as these.

MATTHEW 19:14

Sarah Johnson had one prayer for her son, Robbie: that soon he would find a friend. Sarah and her husband, Karl, had moved to the Pacific Northwest because of work. But in the process, Robbie lost every friend he'd ever had.

Robbie had Down syndrome. Back in Rhode Island, he'd attended a regular public grade school where he took instruction in a special-education classroom. The other students were familiar with him and liked him.

"I have lots of friends," Robbie said with a beam. "Friends are God's way of telling you he loves you."

But ever since the move, Robbie had been quiet and sullen. When asked about his day at school, he'd say, "It was bad. No friends."

Sarah and Karl met with Robbie's teacher, who told them that he wasn't trying to connect. She promised to look for opportunities to get him involved.

That night, Robbie came home from school and said, "I wanna run track. Please, can I, Mom?"

Sarah's heart sank. Even if they were only fifth graders and not very fast, Robbie would be the laughingstock of the school. She bit her lip. *God, give me the words here.* "Son, I'm not sure that track is the best thing for you."

"But I could make friends running." He turned and took four hurried, cloddish steps. "See, Mom. I can run."

Karl thought it might be a good thing. Sarah didn't see how. Still, the next morning she called the office.

"We would welcome him to the team," the school secretary explained. "He would be placed in his own category, for disabled kids. Unless other kids with similar disabilities join track, he'd take first place every time."

When Sarah and Karl explained to Robbie that he'd be on the team, he raised up his hand and flashed a victory sign. "Let's do it."

Every day Robbie came home from practice more excited. When the track season opened, Sarah and Karl took seats in the stands and spotted Robbie in a crowd of kids stretching with one of the coaches. One of the girls noticed that Robbie was stretching over the wrong leg, and she corrected him. Robbie nodded and flashed the girl a smile.

Sarah felt her heart soar. Robbie was making friends.

Later, the announcer called for runners to report for the Special-100. A nervous fluttering rose up in Sarah's stomach. *Please, God. Let him feel good about this.*

"What's that?" Karl pointed as Robbie took his place at the starting line. On either side of him, four other runners lined up, too.

The starting gun sounded, and the runners were off. Robbie led the way, pumping and plodding, and the other able-bodied runners jogged close behind. Robbie crossed the finish line with both arms raised, and the trailing runners enveloped him in a group hug.

Sarah blinked back tears. She looked at Karl and saw him clench his jaw. He cleared his throat and his chin quivered some. "That . . . was amazing."

112

The season continued, and each week the same thing happened. The coach would select the four best performers from the week and allow them the privilege of running in the special race with Robbie. Always they stayed a few feet behind him, pacing him, cheering him on. And always Robbie took first place, fist raised in the air, a victory smile spread across his face.

Finally it was the last meet of the season. Fifteen minutes after the start, the coach ran up to Sarah and Karl in the stands. "We want Robbie to run in the four-hundred relay; is that okay with you?"

"The four-hundred? You mean for special kids?"

"No." The coach grinned. "The four-hundred relay."

"But your team hasn't lost that event all year."

"Exactly," the coach responded. "The other school forfeited. As long as we complete the race, it's an automatic win."

Sarah and Karl gave their blessing, and two hours later Robbie lined up as the first runner in the relay. The gun sounded and Robbie was off, his feet pumping hard. In his hand was the baton. Then, after fifty yards, Robbie tripped and flew forward, hands outstretched. He skidded along the rough track surface and then settled to a stop, motionless.

Sarah was on her feet, stifling a gasp. "Is he okay?"

Karl leaned forward. "Finish the race, Robbie. Come on."

From the three spots along the track where the other three runners were waiting, each of them began running toward Robbie. They helped him to his feet. His knees and upper legs were badly scraped and bleeding; the same with his hands and arms.

When it was obvious that Robbie couldn't keep running, two of the boys made a chair with their arms, and together, carrying Robbie, all four runners trudged to the next station. When they reached it, Robbie handed his baton to one of the boys carrying him.

At that point, the fans rose to their feet, cheering and clapping for the team as they trudged on, all three able-bodied runners shoulder to shoulder, Robbie carried in the middle. When they crossed the finish line, all four runners raised their hands and then formed a group hug, jumping and pumping their fists in the air.

Sarah and Karl had prayed for the acceptance of their son. That prayer was answered a hundredfold. The runners on the field were more than winners. They were a team, and more than that, they were friends.

All the believers were one in heart and mind.

ACTS 4:32

WEEK 18.
A MOTHER WHO
SEES

SCRIPTURE READING:
PROVERBS 31:10–31

I have been reminded of your sincere faith, which first lived in your grandmother Lois and in your mother Eunice and, I am persuaded, now lives in you also.

2 TIMOTHY 1:5

In the town of Bakersfield, California, there was a seven-year-old boy named Luke who played on a Little League baseball team. He was not very athletic and seldom got to play. But his mother, a woman of deep faith, attended every game and cheered for him whether he hit the ball over the fence or struck out.

Life had not been easy for Luke's mother. Sherri Collins married her college sweetheart and they lived what seemed like a storybook life until he was killed in a head-on collision on an icy highway when Luke was three years old.

"I'll never marry anyone else," Sherri told her mother. "No one could ever love me

116

like he did."

"You don't have to convince me." The older woman was also a widow. "Sometimes there's just one special person for a whole lifetime."

Thankfully, Sherri's mother moved in with her after the funeral and helped care for Luke. No matter what trial fell upon the young boy, Sherri had an optimistic way of looking at it.

"That's okay, son," she'd say when Luke came home sad about a situation with a friend. "One day he'll realize how much fun you really are." Or she'd encourage him when he struggled with learning to read. "You can practice reading to me every night, Luke. What a nice way to spend time together!"

Sherri had something deep within her that many mothers understand — an ability to recognize that time is flying by and to make the most of every moment. She knew how quickly life can change.

When Luke turned seven and joined the Little League team, Sherri sensed his struggle, so she researched stories about major leaguers who struggled with the game when they were kids.

"Did you know that the most famous outfielder of all time didn't play ball until he was twelve?" she'd tell him. And together they'd laugh over the possibilities. "One day I'll be cheering from the stands and you'll be suiting up for the big leagues."

Game after game, week after week, his mother came and cheered him on — even if he played only a few minutes at a time. Then one week, Luke came to the game alone. "Coach," he said. "Can I start today? It's really important. Please?"

The coach thought Luke would probably strike out every time. But he also thought of Luke's good sportsmanship during the weeks he'd played but an inning or two.

"Sure," he said, tugging on Luke's red cap. "You can start today. Go get warmed up."

Luke was thrilled and that afternoon he played the game of his life, hitting a home run and two singles and catching the ball that won the game.

The coach was stunned by Luke's performance. "That was a tremendous game," he told the child. "But you've never played like that before. What was the difference?"

Luke smiled and tears began to well up in his brown eyes. "Well, Coach, my dad died a long time ago. My mother was very sick and she was blind. Last week . . . she died." Luke swallowed back the tears. "Today . . .

today was the first time both my parents got to see me play."

He will wipe every tear from their eyes. There will be no more death or mourning or crying or pain, for the old order of things has passed away.

REVELATION 21:4

Week 19.
Angel in the Police Car

SCRIPTURE READING:
1 KINGS 19:1–9

The eyes of the LORD range throughout the earth to strengthen those whose hearts are fully committed to him.

2 CHRONICLES 16:9

The prom was everything Kara Spelling had dreamed it would be. She and her boyfriend danced and laughed and talked until late in the night. Now it was after one in the morning and time to drive back down Interstate 17 to their homes in Camp Verde, Arizona. The prom had been an hour north in Flagstaff and she had driven because her boyfriend didn't have a car.

"Be careful." Her father had kissed her on the forehead before she left. "You look beautiful, honey. But make sure you watch yourself on the way home."

As she climbed into the car, she kicked off her high heels and tossed them into the backseat. Then she smiled at her boyfriend, Thane. "I'm glad we don't drink."

120

"I know," he said. "It's a good feeling . . . having fun and remembering it. Besides," he said, locking his fingers between hers, "I feel good doing the right thing."

Kara nodded and said, "Me, too. You tired?"

Thane yawned. "Yeah, I guess."

"It's an hour to home. Go ahead and sleep."

Five minutes later she entered Interstate 17 North and settled back in her seat. She glanced at Thane, who was already asleep. He wasn't a Christian, but he had started going to church with her and her friends. Every day she prayed that God would get his attention and help him make a decision to believe, and he was close. Why else would he help her serve meals at the homeless shelter?

Kara felt as familiar on this stretch of interstate as she did on the streets around her home. It was wide and safe, utterly remote and monotonous in the pitch dark. She felt herself relax. A yawn came and then another. She turned on the radio and opened the window a crack, which helped for another ten minutes.

But less than halfway home, her eyes closed, her head dropped, then suddenly she jerked it back up again. What had she almost done? She looked at the speedometer — seventy-five miles per hour. If she'd fallen asleep . . . "Come on, Lord," she whispered. "Keep me awake."

Less than a minute later, Kara felt herself nodding off again, but then saw flashing lights in her rearview mirror. Her heart raced as she realized it was a police car. *Great. I must've been swerving.* But she was grateful to be wide awake.

As Kara pulled over, she wondered where the officer had come from. There had been no headlights for miles, and the area was practically deserted. Then she remembered she was driving barefoot, but it was too late to grab her shoes.

"Good evening, Officer," she said as the patrolman came alongside her door and shone a flashlight just high enough so he could see her face.

"Are you all right?" The officer bent over and looked at Kara. Something about his face seemed peaceful, almost unearthly. She noticed his badge number read thirty-seven — the same as her basketball team number.

"Yes, sir. I'm fine."

"Go ahead and put your shoes on. You'll be safer."

Kara felt her heart skip a beat. How did he know about her shoes? Thane reached into the backseat, grabbed her pumps, and handed them to her.

"You've been driving a long way," the officer continued. "You almost fell asleep, didn't you?"

"Why . . . yes." Again Kara was stunned. It was as though he could read her mind. "Maybe you can tell me where the nearest rest stop is."

"Better yet, I'll take you there." The officer smiled and nodded. "You help others all the time. Now it's your turn to get a little assistance. Follow me."

"Wait!" Kara cried out after the man. "How did you know that?"

The officer gave Kara a look that went straight to her soul. "We officers make it our business to know things."

Kara glanced at Thane and saw that he was just as surprised as she was. None of this made sense.

"Kara," Thane said, "how did he know that stuff? It's weird."

Kara followed close behind the patrolman's car all the way to the freeway exit, where it made a sharp right turn. But after making the same turn, Kara could no longer see the police car. "Where did he go?"

"He couldn't have gone far. We saw him turn this way and" — Thane scanned the

parking lot, gas station, and restaurant —
"there's nowhere else he could be."

But he was gone, despite their searching
for him. Suddenly Kara knew. She felt the
hair on her arms rise straight up. "What if
he was an . . . an angel? He saved our lives.
I was falling asleep."

They decided there was only one way to
find out. Kara took out her cell phone and
called the police station. She explained the
situation and was asked for the officer's
badge number. "Thirty-seven."

"Are you sure? We don't have any officers
with a number close to that. Our officers'
badge numbers all have *three* digits."

Kara felt the goose bumps return and
hung up the phone and stared at Thane.
"He must have been an angel. The officers
have three numbers on their badges."

There was a long moment of silence, then
Thane took Kara's hands in his and said
the thing she'd been praying he would say
all year. "I think it's time I made a decision
about God." He kept his eyes on hers, his
expression filled with awe. "I believe, Kara.
I believe."

Now is the time of God's favor, now is the
day of salvation.

2 CORINTHIANS 6:2

124

WEEK 20.
GOD IS IN CONTROL

SCRIPTURE READING:
ECCLESIASTES 3:1–8

When the time drew near for David to die . . .

1 KINGS 2:1

Miranda Thompson sat in the chair beside her mother's bed at the Clark County Nursing Home and watched a dozen birds fluttering outside the window.

"You know what they say about birds, don't you?" the sixty-seven-year-old Miranda asked softly, turning toward her own daughter, Katy.

"No, Mom, what do they say?"

"When birds gather outside the window of a sick person, it means the Lord is ready to call them home."

Miranda held her mother's hand and stroked the wrinkled skin gently. Her mother, Esther, was eighty-six and in a coma. No one expected her to live out the week.

"I love you, Mother," Miranda said

through tears. Then she gazed up, closing her eyes. *Lord, help me accept this. Help me to let my mother go home to you.*

They waited until dinnertime, then Miranda and Katy slowly left, agreeing to meet again the next day.

Miranda drove home in silence, thinking about her mother's decline. Two years earlier the woman had been in good health, living independently in Seattle. Then she began struggling to manage on her own, and finally she had come to live with Miranda and her husband, Bill.

Esther was careful to never impose on the life Miranda and Bill led. She had a sweet disposition and a happy outlook contagious to those around her. Two years passed quickly, and it seemed Esther might live to be a hundred. But while Miranda and Bill were on vacation in Boston, the older woman suffered a series of ministrokes and was placed in intensive care.

Two days into Esther's hospital stay, a nurse accidentally gave her the wrong medication, which slowed Esther's heart and brain activity and sent her into a coma. The doctor explained to Miranda that the nurse would be disciplined for the mistake.

"What does it mean for my mother?" Miranda asked anxiously. "When will she come out of the coma?"

"Mrs. Thompson, because of her condition and age, she might not come out of it. She might go downhill."

Miranda nodded, trying not to cry. "But if she comes out of it soon, she still might make a recovery. Right?"

"Honestly, I don't think it's likely."

When Esther remained in the coma for four days, the hospital staff decided there was nothing more they could do for her, so she was moved to the nursing home.

Two weeks passed and now, as Miranda drove home, she felt terribly cheated. Her mother had been healthy and witty and might have had years left. Miranda was doing her best to avoid blaming the nurse.

"Lord, help me to understand why this happened," she prayed softly. "It doesn't seem fair that Mother should be cheated of her last years of life."

When Miranda got home it was nearly dusk, and the house felt cold and lonely. Just three weeks earlier her mother would have been there. "I need to get outside before I work myself into a full-blown depression," Miranda said to herself.

Finding her gardening gloves, she went out to her beautiful garden in the front yard. Working steadily among the flowers, she heard a man's voice nearby.

"My, your flowers are so lovely."

Miranda looked up and saw, standing on the sidewalk, a tall man holding the leash of a beautiful little dog. Miranda smiled sadly. Her mother loved dogs.

"Thank you," Miranda said, leaning back on her heels and looking into the man's face. She had lived here for thirty-five years but had never seen him before.

"They aren't as pretty as they could be if I had more time to take care of them," she said. "My mother's sick."

The man gazed at Miranda kindly. There was something unearthly about him, a glow almost.

"She was given the wrong medication and now she's dying. I want to be with her as much as possible."

She felt the tears welling up in her eyes again.

"Don't worry about your mother," the man said, his voice strong and gentle. "God is in control."

The man continued to watch her. How strange that someone she didn't know would offer words of wisdom.

"Sir, where do you live?" she finally asked.

The man said nothing, but pointed upward. Miranda looked toward the sky instinctively. When she glanced back, the man and his dog were nowhere to be seen.

Miranda was shocked. There was no way they could have vanished so quickly. Then she realized that she hadn't seen him arrive. He had just appeared with words of encouragement and then disappeared.

"God is in control." Miranda pondered the truth in the man's words and found that as the evening passed she felt less burdened.

The next morning, Miranda received a phone call from the nursing home. "Mrs. Thompson, your mother has died very peacefully in her sleep."

Miranda shut her eyes as one hand flew to her mouth, and she felt a sob catch in her throat. Then, she remembered the man in the garden. A sense of peace came over her, and suddenly she knew her prayers had been answered. She bowed her head.

"Dear God, I understand now. There are no accidents where you're concerned. Mother didn't die because of the nurse or the medication; she died because you were ready to bring her home. You are in control. I understand that better now, Lord. And I thank you."

The LORD gave and the LORD has taken

away; may the name of the LORD be praised.

JOB 1:21

WEEK 21.
ON A FOREIGN BATTLEFIELD

SCRIPTURE READING:
EXODUS 17:8–16

Greater love has no one than this, that he lay down his life for his friends.

JOHN 15:13

Ben Wiggins had two sisters, but the first died at birth, and the second died tragically at age two. He grew up as an only child and never forgot his parents' loss.

"Don't worry, Mom," he'd tell her. "You'll always have me around. I'm not going anywhere."

Ben's mother, Sarah, would grin sadly and say, "God has taken two of my babies home. But he knows how much a mother can handle, Ben. You're the one he left for me and your father."

But when Ben turned eighteen, he enlisted in the U.S. Army. Not long after, the Gulf War began, and Ben was assigned a place on the front line. The idea of losing Ben terrified his parents, but they prayed constantly.

131

"Please, God, let us know when he needs our prayers," Sarah would pray each night. "And bring Ben home safely to us. He's all we have left, Lord."

The initial drive of the Gulf War figured to be the most dangerous. As Ben waited and took his position, he silently prayed, *God, be with me. Let me survive.*

When the moment of battle came, Ben pressed across the border of Iraq, shoulder to shoulder with hundreds of Army men. The battle that ensued was intense and fast. One hour led to two, and it looked as though the U.S. troops would be wildly successful.

During a brief lull in the action, Ben was resting for a second when he felt someone grab his arm. He spun around and looked straight into the eyes of an Iraqi soldier, whose gun was aimed directly at Ben's face.

In angry, short bursts the Iraqi shouted words Ben didn't understand. He stood there, afraid to move, when the man suddenly hit him on the side of the face with the butt of the rifle and pointed in the opposite direction from his squad. Ben had no choice but to start walking.

God! Help me! Please . . .

Several times over the next few minutes Ben considered shouting for help. It was clear that his squad hadn't noticed his disappearance and he was on his own. Stopping on a sandy desert bluff, again the soldier barked something at Ben. Ben blinked, not knowing what to do; then the soldier kicked him and pointed to the ground. Fearing for his life, Ben lowered himself to the dusty ground and was kicked again, forcing him to lie on his stomach. *This is it, God. I'm not going to make it without a miracle.* A dozen memories flashed through his mind, and one was of his parents praying for him.

His parents! That was it! He knew his mother was praying for him every day. The Iraqi soldier barked something else and dug the tip of the rifle into the back of his skull. Ben drew a shaky breath, afraid it would be his last. Then he closed his eyes and prayed as he'd never done before: *God, please let my mother know I'm in danger. She should be praying for me.*

Moments earlier, across the world in Austin, Texas, Sarah Wiggins sat up straight in bed and screamed. "Al, wake up!" she cried as her husband snapped awake.

"What is it?" he asked breathlessly.

"It's Ben. He's hurt or in trouble. I can feel it."

Al sighed and relaxed somewhat. "Sarah, he's in Kuwait. There's no way to know that."

Sarah nodded, her heart racing. "Yes, Al. I prayed that God would let me know when he needed help. Why else would I wake up in the middle of the night?"

Al considered that, then spoke tenderly to calm his wife. "If he's in trouble, what can we do about it?"

"We can pray."

"Okay." Al nodded and took his wife's hands in his.

Sarah bowed her head and closed her eyes as she began to pray out loud. "Lord, you know where Ben is and what he needs. Please help him. Whatever danger he's in, please help him. In your holy name, amen."

Back in Kuwait, at that same instant, Ben heard a distinct voice speaking near his ear. "Don't worry. You are not going to die today. God is with you."

Ben looked around, but other than the Iraqi solder, he was completely alone on the desert bluff. The realization sent chills down his arms, even though the tip of the soldier's rifle still dug into his skull. *You're here, God. I hear you. I feel your presence. I beg you for a miracle, God . . . please.*

The moment Ben finished praying, the Iraqi soldier shouted something, then yanked the gun away from Ben's head and inexplicably ran down the embankment.

Ben could hardly breathe. He was alive! And for the moment, the danger had passed. *Thank you, God. Whatever just happened . . . thank you.* With slow, cautious movements, he stood up and started across the desert. Ducking low, he ran with every bit of strength he had until he was safely among U.S. soldiers again.

Two weeks later, Ben was back at base and allowed to call home. As his story tumbled out, Sarah felt chill bumps along her spine.

"When did it happen?" she asked. "The exact time."

"About two in the morning your time."

Sarah's hand flew to her mouth. "I was praying for you, Ben. God woke me up and had me pray for you."

Across the miles in Kuwait, Ben's heart soared at his mother's statement. "I knew it. I prayed for a miracle, Mom. I asked God to let you know I was in trouble. And that's just what he did."

As for me, far be it from me that I should sin against the LORD by failing to pray for

135

you. And I will teach you the way that is good and right.

1 SAMUEL 12:23

WEEK 22.
THE RIGHT PLACE AT THE RIGHT TIME

SCRIPTURE READING:
DEUTERONOMY 24:17–22

I was a stranger and you invited me in, I needed clothes and you clothed me, I was sick and you looked after me.

MATTHEW 25:35–36

Sam Sturgell went into family law because he believed that with God's help, an attorney could wreak miracles and goodness rather than destruction between a couple and their children. Every day, Sam prayed that the Lord would use his talents to bring about his purposes in the lives of the people Sam worked for.

One afternoon he took a call from Lucy Manning, a former classmate in law school who had dropped out to pursue her love for adventure as a flight attendant. She had met a windsurfer in Portland and fallen in love. Everything was perfect until she wound up pregnant and her boyfriend had no interest in fatherhood.

Lucy felt that adoption would be the

ultimate gift. Yes, the pregnancy would set her back in her career. But somewhere in the Portland area, there had to be a couple desperate for a child.

She called Sam and explained the situation. He lined up several portfolios of families. Lucy picked a couple with a five-year-old boy and the inability to have more children. She barely noticed a small line in the couple's dossier: *Healthy child only.*

The week that Lucy was scheduled to deliver, Anthony and Amber Aarons had been approved for adoption. They had contacted Sam Sturgell and were waiting for a baby. But not just any baby.

The week before, the Aaronses were at a nephew's soccer game when they noticed a boy who had a hand with no fingers. The boy blocked one goal attempt after another while his family cheered for him. Everything about the scene took Anthony Aarons back.

Anthony had been born with a cleft palate, in which the tissue between the nose and the lip doesn't develop properly. By the time surgery had been performed, the teasing from other kids had taken its toll. Anthony's confidence was almost nonexistent, but it was made worse by his father.

His parents divorced when Anthony was ten. After that his father would visit two or three times a year. Once he overheard his father tell his mother that he looked terrible and needed another surgery. Other times Anthony would catch his father studying his upper lip area with a disgusted look on his face.

Anthony's saving grace had been his mother's love. She took him to church and taught him to believe in the plans God had for his life. She was the first on her feet to applaud when he graduated with a master's degree in counseling. His life would be a wonderful one because she believed in him all along.

Those memories were strong as Anthony watched the little boy playing soccer. The child beamed with confidence, convinced — because of the obvious love from his family — that he could do anything he set his mind to do.

On the way home, Amber said, "I can't stop thinking about that special boy."

"Me either."

"Like maybe God's trying to tell us we're supposed to adopt a child with special needs?"

The question rattled the walls of Anthony's soul. It was exactly what he'd been thinking. "Is that really what you've been thinking?"

"Yes. I want to be that mother, cheering for a child who might not get cheers otherwise."

That Monday, Anthony called Sam and explained their change of plans. "We'll probably go through the state. Most private adoptions deal with healthy kids, right?"

Sam replied, "Most of the time. But once in a while God has a miracle up his sleeve, a reason why a couple like you changes your mind about wanting a healthy child. Let's go ahead and contact the state. But in the meantime, I'll keep your file on my desk and pray."

Anthony and Amber began to pray that the Lord would bring them the right little boy or girl, someone whose life they could truly impact.

A few days later, Lucy Manning went into labor. The hour the baby was born Sam took the call from Lucy, and she was crying. "Sam . . . there's a problem. The baby has . . . a cleft palate. Please pray for us."

Sam's heart ached for Lucy and the baby, and for the adoptive couple. They wanted a healthy baby, nothing else. A call to the couple made the situation sure.

Sam was hanging up the phone when his eyes fell on the Aaronses' file. Of course. Not only would they take a baby with a disability, but they wanted such a child. He grinned as his trembling fingers dialed their number. He realized something he hadn't considered before. Though it was barely noticeable, Anthony had also been a victim of a cleft palate. Then he heard Anthony answer, "Hello."

"Anthony, it's Sam. I think we're on the brink of a miracle here."

"Okay, Sam, what's up?"

"If you could have a child with any certain type of disability, what would you choose?"

It was a strange question, but Anthony didn't hesitate. "I was born with a cleft palate; you probably know that. I guess I would understand that best."

Sam had a lump in his throat too big to slip words past. When he could finally talk, he said, "Anthony, God's brought a baby into the world that couldn't belong to anyone but you and Amber."

Eight years have passed since then. Amber and Anthony adopted little Randall James, who has a strong spirit, something instilled in him by his parents' faith and determination. That spirit shows up most on the soccer field where Randy is one of the top defenders. And his parents? The best cheering section of all.

Your love has given me great joy and encouragement.

PHILEMON 1:7

WEEK 23.
NEVER FEAR

SCRIPTURE READING:
ACTS 12:1–19

See that you do not look down on one of these little ones. For I tell you that their angels in heaven always see the face of my Father in heaven.

MATTHEW 18:10

It was the last day of school and Melba Stevens was waiting for her seven-year-old son, Mark, to come home. She sat in a chair by the window and thought about the conversation she'd had with the child that morning.

"Mom, are there really guardian angels?"

Melba had smiled. Lately Mark had been almost constantly curious about spiritual matters and this was merely the next in a list of questions he'd asked lately. "Yes, son. There really are."

"I'll bet my angel's huge, don't you think so?"

Melba had stifled a laugh. "Why?"

"Because I'm the kind of kid who needs a

143

really huge angel, that's why."

Mark's eyes had grown large when he talked about his overly large guardian angel. *Silly boy,* she thought.

Mark was their only child, a special gift considering Melba's fertility problems. Doctors thought she'd never be able to conceive and when Mark was born they had to perform a hysterectomy. There would be no other children, but that was okay with Melba and her husband. Mark was a very special child and more than enough to fill their home with love and joy and laughter. "Hurry up and get home, Mark . . . your mama's waiting," she whispered.

Just two blocks away, Mark Stevens was in a particularly giddy mood. "Summer's here!" he shouted.

"Yahoo!" his friend shouted, looking at the four busy lanes of traffic ahead of them. "Watch this!" With that he ran across the lanes and jumped onto the opposite curb. "Come on!" the boy yelled. "Don't be a chicken."

Mark hesitated. His mother had forbidden him to cross the street by himself, but . . . he blinked hard. "Okay!" Without checking for traffic, he made his dash.

Suddenly Mark heard the children behind him scream and he froze in the middle of the road. A fast car was coming straight for him.

"Mom!" he screamed. And then there was a sickening thud.

Back at home, Melba felt a ripple of panic course through her. Mark was never late. She slipped on a pair of sandals and began walking toward the school.

Hearing sirens, she picked up her pace. She saw an ambulance and fire engine and a cluster of people gathered around a figure on the ground. *Dear God, don't let it be Mark.*

Melba began to run, convincing herself it couldn't be her precious boy. But as she ran a memory came to mind of a bad dream Mark had suffered recently.

"I'm scared, Mom. Like something bad is going to happen to me. I don't want to be alone."

"Mark," she said, "you have nothing to be afraid of. God has placed a guardian angel by your side to watch over you while you sleep and to protect you by day."

That conversation must have sparked the one she and Mark had earlier that morning.

Melba was almost to the accident scene when she realized the child on the ground was Mark. "Dear God!" she screamed as she pressed her way to the front of the crowd. Terror racked her body. "Is he okay?"

"He's conscious," one of the paramedics said. "This is incredible. The kid shouldn't even be alive."

Mark could hear the paramedics and his mother in the distance. Lying on the ground, not moving, he remembered flying through the air. But when he'd hit the ground, there had been no pain — as if someone had set him gently down on the pavement. He looked up and saw a circle of people working on him.

"Check his pulse and reflexes," someone shouted.

"Don't move him yet! Check for head injuries."

Mark looked around and suddenly gasped. Hovering directly over him and gazing into his eyes was a gigantic man with golden hair. The man was smiling, and Mark understood that he was going to be okay. As the man faded from view, Mark's mother stepped closer.

Melba watched a smile come over her son's face and she knelt at his side. "Mark, are you okay?" she cried.

Mark blinked, his face pale but otherwise unharmed. "I'm fine, Mom. I saw my guardian angel and I was right. He's so huge you wouldn't believe it."

Hope surged through Melba as a paramedic pushed her gently back from the scene. "He's suffered a serious blow. He could have back and neck injuries, any number of problems. You can ride along in the ambulance."

Melba began to weep quietly as they loaded her son into the ambulance. Before they pulled away, she heard a policeman say to four firemen, "The car must have been doing forty-plus, and the boy sailed through the air. Came down on his head and there's no blood. I've never seen anything like it."

Melba felt a tingling sensation pass over her. *No blood? How was that possible?* Then she remembered Mark's words: "I saw my guardian angel."

At the hospital, doctors checked to determine whether Mark had feeling in all parts of his body. "By all accounts," one doctor said, "he should have died at the scene. And I can't even find a scratch or bruise."

Within an hour the doctor was stunned that the results of a dozen different tests were completely normal. The boy had no internal injuries.

"My guardian angel saved me," Mark explained. "That's why I needed a huge angel, Mom."

Today, Melba remains grateful for the precious faith of her only child. After the accident, his young faith became vitally real, propelling him through his teenage years and into a career as a youth pastor, working with kids who pepper him with as many questions about spiritual matters as he once had for his mother.

The angel of the LORD encamps around those who fear him, and he delivers them.
PSALM 34:7

WEEK 24.
MY FATHER, MY FRIEND

SCRIPTURE READING:
PSALM 23

Praise be to the God and Father of our Lord Jesus Christ, the Father of compassion and the God of all comfort, who comforts us in all our troubles . . .
                    2 CORINTHIANS 1:3–4

From the time she was little, Tina Ewing had always been close to her father. In middle school, she was chosen for an advanced-level all-star soccer team, and every weekend he would accompany her as they traveled to tournaments, cheering his encouragement. When she got involved in volleyball and basketball in her sophomore year, he was at every game.

Tina's mother was a bank executive and kept long hours. Her father was self-employed and could work his schedule around her activities. He would take her sailing and rollerblading, and he often told her about God's plans for her life — great plans.

"Never doubt for a minute how much God loves you." He'd grin at her. "Get that part right and everything in life will fall into place."

That year, during an essay contest to describe her best friend, Tina wrote, "My dad's my best friend. He understands me better than anyone else."

Tina was eighteen when her father began to lose weight and cough. After three months, a doctor gave the family the dreaded diagnosis — lung cancer that had already spread to his liver. Two months later he was hospitalized and called Tina to his bedside.

"Don't blame . . . God for this, sweetheart." He managed a smile, though he was breathless from the effort of talking. "God's calling me home. It's part of his plan, for whatever reason."

Two weeks later he died. It wasn't until after his funeral service that she broke down and wept. Her mother sat on the bed beside her. "He'll always be with you, baby. Always."

But for months, Tina couldn't shake the dark cloud his absence had left. There were times when she didn't go to school. Calls to her mother didn't help. Counseling sessions did nothing. She lost weight and dark circles appeared beneath her once-bright eyes.

Tina knew she needed a divine intervention, God's miraculous power, but how could she begin a conversation with God when he was the very one who had let her father die? She hated that thought, but it didn't go away. And as the months passed, she could not escape or explain the emptiness inside her. She barely graduated from high school and spent the summer in depression.

In the fall, sometime near the anniversary of her father's death, Tina and her friends Diane and Lora decided to hike along a lake that had been one of her father's favorites. Her friends said it was time to do it, but she dreaded the memories. *God, give me the strength.*

For nearly thirty minutes the three friends walked in silence, each lost in her own thoughts. One after another the memories of her father bombarded Tina with an almost physical force. They kept walking, and Tina could practically hear her father's voice as they approached the steepest hill. There, at the top, was a bench where Tina and her father had often sat and talked.

Refusing to give in to her overwhelming feelings of grief, Tina looked up and saw a tall man in jeans and a T-shirt standing at the top of the hill looking out at the lake. He looked exactly like her father. She gasped, but her friends didn't seem to notice. Tina stared at the man, and suddenly she felt a burden being lifted from her shoulders. When they were just ten yards from the man, he turned toward Tina and smiled the same warm and reassuring smile that had once belonged to her father.

Tina's friends still seemed oblivious to the man and walked past without stopping. She paused and stared into his eyes. He winked once, smiled again, and then slowly turned back toward the lake.

She seemed to know, instinctively, that there was no need to question the man or engage in dialogue. A peaceful remembrance washed over her, and after months of grieving, she felt at peace with herself.

At the bottom of the hill, she asked her friends to stop. "Did you see that man at the top of the hill?"

"What man?" Diane's expression was blank.

"Yeah, who?" Lora asked. "We've been the only ones on the trail all day."

"No, seriously. Back there on the hill. The guy in the jeans. He looked just like my —" Tina stopped short. Her friends would think she was crazy if she explained it. Besides, if they hadn't seen anyone, then . . . Tina felt another wave of peace. "Never mind," she said. "Must've been my imagination."

Tina kept the incident to herself. Regardless of what anyone else would say to doubt it, from that point on Tina was convinced that an angel, somehow cloaked in the appearance of her father, had been there. Perhaps he would always be there, watching over her.

This notion was confirmed five years later when Tina was working in Los Angeles near the Federal Building. Pausing at a curb, waiting for the light to change, she suddenly felt a firm hand on her shoulder that pulled her away from the curb with a force so strong it nearly knocked her to the ground. At the exact same instant, a city bus jumped the curb directly where she had been standing. If she had remained standing there, she'd have been killed.

Tina turned at once to thank the person who had rescued her, but there was no one within fifty feet of her. Again she felt an overwhelming sense of peace and reassurance.

"The Bible says God assigns his angels to watch over us," Tina says now. "He did that for me when I was a teenager, devastated by my father's death. And he does it still."

Do not fear, for I am with you; do not be dismayed, for I am your God. I will strengthen you and help you; I will uphold you with my righteous right hand.

ISAIAH 41:10

WEEK 25.
A DREAM COME
TRUE

SCRIPTURE READING:
2 KINGS 4:8–37

The blind receive sight, the lame walk, those who have leprosy are cured, the deaf hear, the dead are raised, and the good news is preached to the poor.

MATTHEW 11:5

When Angie Bauer became pregnant after having three sons, Ben Bauer said, "I wish we could have a blonde, blue-eyed little girl."

Angie laughed. There were no blonde, blue-eyed people in either of their families. None. "Good luck."

When Angie was four months pregnant, after a routine ultrasound, Angie's doctor ushered her into his office and closed the door. "Something has shown up and I'd like you to see a specialist."

She searched his face. "That sounds serious."

"Something is developing at the base of the baby's neck. It looks like cystic hy-

155

groma, a rare condition involving fluid buildup in the lymph system."

"What does that mean for the baby?"

"Let's see what the specialist says first."

A week later, Angie and Ben drove to Cleveland, where the diagnosis was the same.

"She has cystic hygroma, which is a rare —"

"She?" Ben interrupted the doctor.

"Yes, a girl with a very rare condition. Her lymph system is not redistributing fluids throughout her body. Instead fluid is gathering at the base of the skull and developing into sacs that will eventually circle her neck and choke her to death. I'm afraid she won't live more than a couple of months at most."

"What can you do? Surgery?" Ben was devastated.

"I'm sorry. I suggest you terminate the pregnancy."

Angie's eyes grew wide. "You mean abort?"

"Mrs. Bauer, your baby will die anyway. It'll be much easier if you go ahead and terminate now."

Angie sat up straight. "Doctor, we won't abort this baby. My little girl won't die at my hands."

"It is not our policy to do abortions.

However, there is no reason to continue the pregnancy."

"If I continue the pregnancy, am I in any danger?"

"No, none at all."

"Then I want to continue it."

"You must understand that if by some slim chance she survives the pregnancy, we must suction fluid from the sacs during labor before she can come through the birth canal, which will make it long and hard. If she survives the delivery, the sacs must be removed by surgery immediately and there may be other organs that are drowning in fluid. And if she still survives, she probably will be mentally handicapped. This is a condition that often goes along with cystic hygroma in female babies."

"Then that's the chance we'll take," Angie said. "Sometimes you just have to trust God on these matters."

The drive home was one of the longest in their lives.

"Why us, Ben?" Angie cried, beginning to sob. She felt helpless and completely brokenhearted.

"Angie, we need to pray and have everyone we know pray. God can heal her, honey."

They told their boys about the baby's

problem that night. Bo, their five-year-old, said, "We're asking Jesus to help." After that, every night the boys prayed, "Dear God, please make our sister be fine. Don't let her die."

Sunday came and Ben and Angie went in front of their church family and asked for prayers for healing. Throughout the congregation people were crying with them, and the praying began immediately. A group of grandmothers at the church made the unborn baby their top prayer concern. They contacted other women they knew at other churches and the prayer chain grew. In addition, Ben's parents and Angie's parents prayed constantly for God to work a miracle.

Six weeks passed and Angie and Ben returned for another appointment. After Angie was examined by the specialist, she looked intently at him. "What are the odds that this baby will survive the entire pregnancy?"

"Less than one percent. If she survives the delivery, the odds get worse from that point on."

Angie left the doctor's office and walked to the room where sonograms were performed. Ben waited while a technician scanned Angie's abdomen. Minutes passed and she wondered why it was taking so long.

Eventually, the technician said, "I'm going to take these pictures to my supervisor. Wait here."

Alone in the dark room, Angie silently began to pray, repeating Scriptures that promised hope and peace. Ten minutes later the technician returned and said, "Okay, no more pictures. The doctor wants to see you."

Angie explained what was happening to Ben as they walked to the doctor's office. After they were seated, he strode into the room smiling.

"There is no medical explanation for this," he said, his words tumbling out, "but the fluid sacs have almost completely disappeared and the fluid is being redistributed in a normal manner. She will definitely live through the pregnancy."

Angie released a cry and collapsed in Ben's arms.

Ben gasped. "Hundreds of people have prayed."

The doctor shrugged. "Well, she will still probably have Turner's syndrome and still require surgery. She will most likely have mental retardation."

Angie looked up. "God doesn't do half a miracle."

"Don't get your hopes up. The damage

has already been done. I suggest you have an amniocentesis done to obtain information about the baby's chromosomes."

"There's a risk of miscarriage with that procedure and knowing the baby's condition won't help her," Angie said calmly. "We'll prepare by praying about it."

"Okay, but when she's born please have her tested and send the results to my office."

When they left the hospital, Ben grinned. "God is giving me a little blonde, blue-eyed angel after all."

"Honey, look in the mirror and ask yourself if she could have anything but your dark hair and eyes."

Weeks passed and then months. At the end of Angie's eighth month of pregnancy, test results were perfect. She was told, "Surgery will not be necessary." The prayers continued. Finally, a week before her due date, Angie went into labor and Maggie was born. Tests were done immediately and her physical examination proved her to be completely healthy.

Two weeks later the blood work came back. Maggie's chromosomes were completely normal. The doctor held one final meeting with the couple. "I want you to know," he said, his eyes misty, "Maggie has changed the way I'll advise patients with this disorder. If you'd followed my advice . . . I thank God you didn't."

As Maggie grew, the only sign that remained of her ordeal was a slight thickening at the base of her neck. Once, when Maggie was five, Angie was struggling with the top button of the little girl's blouse.

"You'll always have a hard time with those top buttons because your neck is a little thicker than some," she said. "That's God's reminder that you were a miracle."

Maggie nodded. "Daddy says I'm his miracle baby."

Angie pulled her daughter tight. "Yes, honey. You're our little blonde, blue-eyed miracle baby."

We live by faith, not by sight.
                                    2 CORINTHIANS 5:7

Week 26.
A Forever Home

SCRIPTURE READING:
ESTHER 2

Religion that God our Father accepts as pure and faultless is this: to look after orphans and widows in their distress and to keep oneself from being polluted by the world.

JAMES 1:27

Christopher Owens studied the faces looking back at him. They were all foster kids — children abandoned or neglected or taken away from their parents. Their week at Second Chances Summer Camp each July was probably the highlight of the year for most of them. He drew a deep breath. "My message for you is simple. No matter how it feels right now, God has a plan for your life."

Then he allowed himself to go back twenty-plus years to the summer when he was six years old. He had been an only child, the son of a drug-dealer father and an alcoholic mother. The shady dealings of his parents and the strange people who came and went from his house had seemed like a normal life.

Yes, once in a while he would watch his father push his mother around or slap her in the face. Sometimes his parents talked about getting rid of him. And sometimes his crying mother would pull him onto her lap and rock him. "I'm sorry, Christopher. I've told Jesus I'm sorry. This isn't any kind of life for a little boy. God forgive me."

Then things got out of hand. His father fired a gun at a mean guy who stopped by the house. And somehow his mother got in the way of the bullets. She fell down a few feet from Christopher and never got up again.

"Mommy!" Christopher could still feel the way the words felt in his heart and on his lips that day. "Mommy, wake up! Please, Mommy!"

The whole time, his daddy sat at the table with his head in his hands, crying and mumbling something about his life being over.

Police officers rushed through the door, then an ambulance pulled up outside his house. He never saw either of his parents again. The social worker explained the situation to him that night after he was taken to a big house. His mommy was dead, gone to be with Jesus. His father had gone to jail.

And Christopher would stay with the nice family in the big house — at least for now, until the social services department could find someone to adopt Christopher and make him their very own — his forever family.

The Owens family was wonderful. But Christopher didn't dare hope the family might one day be his own. His social worker told him from the beginning that the situation was only temporary.

That summer, the Owenses sent him to the Second Chance Summer Camp in Kansas City, Missouri. By then, Christopher was desperately afraid and lonely. He wanted his mother in the worst way. Things had been bad back then, but at least he'd had a family, a home to call his own.

"Christopher," Mrs. Owens said, "God has a plan for your life. While you're at camp, pray that God will make that plan clear to all of us."

It was at camp that Christopher learned the message of God's love and his second chances for all people. For the first time in his life, Christopher wasn't afraid or lonely or anxious. Jesus was on his side, looking out for him, walking beside him. Maybe everything would be all right, after all.

Before he left, he got down on his knees. The counselor had told him to ask Jesus for the best dreams in his heart. He gulped twice and began the most important prayer he'd ever prayed. "Please, God, let the Owens family be my forever family."

When Christopher came home, balloons filled the front yard and ribbons were strung between the trees. On the house was a banner that read: "Welcome to your forever home, Christopher!"

Christopher looked from Mrs. Owens to Mr. Owens, his little heart racing within him. "What does it mean?"

"We've been trying to adopt you." Mr. Owens put his arm around Christopher.

Christopher held his breath, afraid he might wake up and find he was only dreaming.

"While you were gone, the paperwork came through." Mrs. Owens kissed him on the forehead. "Would you like to be our son forever, Christopher?"

He wanted to shout to the heavens, "Yes!" But tears blurred his eyes and his words stuck in his throat. His heart was happier than it had ever been, even if the words wouldn't come. And so he threw his arms around Mrs. Owens's neck, and then Mr. Owens's neck.

Christopher's life was forever changed. His faith in God grew, and there seemed to be truth in everything the camp counselor had said. Jesus did hear his prayers; he did care about a lost little boy who didn't have a home or a hope in the world.

The years found Christopher growing in the grace of God with every year. He was always top of his class, an athlete with a kind, compassionate heart and an enormous love for his family. As he set off for college, his adopted parents told him he could become whatever he dreamed of becoming.

Christopher's goal never wavered once through college. He was hired a few months after his graduation to be a counselor at the Second Chance Summer Camp. Today, Christopher runs the camp and every summer he shares with hopeless, lonely little boys the same message someone once shared with him.

His words were strong as he finished his talk that afternoon. "And so, boys, believe it more than you've ever believed anything in your life. God has a plan for you, a good plan to give you a hope and a future. The same way he had a plan for me."

The LORD was with Samuel as he grew

166

up, and he let none of his words fall to the ground.

1 SAMUEL 3:19

WEEK 27.
RETURNING THE FAVOR

SCRIPTURE READING:
ACTS 9:36–43

God is not unjust; he will not forget your work and the love you have shown him as you have helped his people and continue to help them.

HEBREWS 6:10

Rob Garrett and his wife and daughters were happy and healthy, living in Thousand Oaks, California, where they were involved in their church and every day seemed better than the last. Then six-year-old Alicia came down with a series of unexplained fevers. A series of blood tests led to a diagnosis worse than anything they'd imagined. Alicia had leukemia.

"It's advancing quickly," the doctor told them. "She'll need a bone marrow transplant within a month. We'll test your family members first, but if there's no match, it's time for drastic measures."

Rob could barely breathe. "Drastic measures?"

168

"Yes. Time to pray for a miracle."

Some two thousand miles away, Peter Hickman was the president of a major division of a nationally known biotech company and married to the woman of his dreams, with two children. He wasn't a praying man, but lately he'd taken to thanking God and asking for just one thing: that he might find Rob Garrett.

Thirteen years earlier Peter had been the least popular boy at a private high school in Detroit. He wore tortoiseshell glasses and when he tried to discuss algebraic theories with his classmates, they only laughed. He was the outcast on campus.

But one girl — Maryanne Ellis — had captured his heart. She had blonde hair halfway to her waist and was the prettiest girl he'd ever seen. But she had never noticed him.

Then one day, Rob Garrett, the star football running back, approached him and said, "Hey, Hickman. I got a favor to ask. Can we can get together and study?"

Was this a joke? "Why me?"

"Because I need an A in this class to get a scholarship, okay? Will you help me or not?"

Peter agreed and the two began to study three times a week at the school library. As the weeks passed, Peter began to think of Rob as a friend. And every once in a while Maryanne would walk past and Peter would blush.

"She's hot, Hickman. I don't know if you're her type."

"Yeah . . . she's out of my league."

One day when they'd finished that same exchange, Rob said, "Maybe we can get you somewhere with Maryanne." Rob first took Peter to the mall for a set of contacts and a haircut. Next they picked up new jeans and sweaters. Rob taught Peter how to walk and stand with more confidence, relaxed and in control. Eye contact and a slower conversational style were the final touches. Peter looked like a different guy.

A week later, Rob introduced Peter to Maryanne.

"Hi." Her smile was somewhat shy. "Are you new?"

Peter wasn't sure what to say. "Sort of."

After that, Rob flagged Maryanne down every day, and one day Peter got up the nerve to ask her to a dance.

Without hesitation she nodded. "Sure, I'd love to."

Fourteen years later, Peter and Maryanne were happier than ever. But at least once a week he wondered about Rob Garrett.

Wasn't there something he could do to thank the guy for all he'd done? Then one night Peter did an Internet search that turned up an e-mail address. Peter sent a quick note, stating that if the recipient was indeed Rob Garrett from St. Thomas High School, he'd like to talk to him.

The next day, in his online mailbox, Peter found a response from Rob's wife. Yes, Peter had reached the right person, but Rob was very busy. She included their phone number and address.

Peter nearly jumped from his seat. He had a business trip that weekend, only an hour from Rob's house. "Maryanne" — he grinned at her — "I think I'm taking a side trip this time."

Rob was nearly at the end of his rope. Neither he nor his wife nor their oldest daughter had matched Alicia's blood type. The chance of a match outside the family was one in ten thousand. The national donor bank had nothing for their daughter, and Alicia's cancer was advancing at an alarming rate.

As they drove home, Alicia fell asleep, and Rob and his wife prayed quietly. "We need a miracle, God."

When they pulled up in front of their

house, a sedan was parked outside. As they climbed out of their car, the door of the sedan opened and a man stood up and waved. "Rob Garrett?"

Rob studied the man. "Yes, how can I help you?"

"Rob, it's me! Peter Hickman!"

"Peter Hickman? What are you doing here?"

Peter walked up and shook Rob's hand. "I've wanted to find you for the past fourteen years, Rob."

Rob wished he felt more upbeat. But as his wife carried Alicia into the house, he felt like crying.

As the two men headed for the house, Peter gushed on about his happy life with Maryanne and his children. "All these years I wanted to thank you. I kept wishing there was some way I could pay you back."

"Don't worry about it, Peter." Then they sat down in the living room. "I'm glad it worked out so well."

"How about you, Rob? How're things with you?"

At first, Rob didn't want to talk. After all, the sooner Peter was gone, the sooner Rob could get back to Alicia. But in that moment, these words of Jesus came to mind: "Where two or more are gathered, there I

172

am also."

"Rob? Are you okay?"

"No." The word was lost in a stifled sob. "Not really."

Peter put his arm on Rob's shoulder. "What's wrong?"

Rob told him everything about Alicia's situation.

When Rob finished, Peter stood. "I'm going to have them draw blood. I could be a match. I have to find out."

The idea seemed almost ludicrous; but it couldn't hurt. Rob went with Peter to the hospital and his blood was drawn. Peter said he needed the results as soon as possible because he was from out of town. The nurse promised to phone the results in an hour.

They were just finishing dinner when the phone rang and Rob answered.

"Mr. Garrett?" The voice was brimming with excitement. "Mr. Hickman is a match. A perfect match!"

Rob fell in slow motion to his knees and hung his head.

"What is it, Rob?" Peter touched Rob's arm.

Rob couldn't talk. He was on holy ground. Hours after he and his wife had prayed for a miracle, a man he hadn't seen in fourteen years walked up and was their daughter's perfect match.

The phone fell to the floor, and Rob vaguely noticed his wife picking it up. In a matter of seconds, she relayed the good news to Peter, and the three of them hugged and shouted and thanked God.

The surgery took place later that week, and no one was surprised when the transplant was a complete success. The miracle that had begun when Rob stepped into Peter's life and helped him meet Maryanne was finally complete. Only God could have brought the two together at that time, when Peter might repay his friend by giving away a part of himself and in the process save Rob's little girl.

> May the LORD repay you for what you have done. May you be richly rewarded by the LORD, the God of Israel, under whose wings you have come to take refuge.
>
> RUTH 2:12

WEEK 28.
A DOUBLE MIRACLE
SCRIPTURE READING:
JOB 42:7–17

Confess your sins to each other and pray
for each other so that you may be healed.
The prayer of a righteous man is powerful
and effective.

JAMES 5:16

Other than one troubled relationship, life
couldn't have been better for Tracy Black.
She and her husband, Paul, had three
children and a beautiful home on three
acres, and she loved everything about her
life. But thoughts of her broken friendship
with Anna Ritter had often haunted her over
the past five years.

As Tracy worked in her garden that summer afternoon, she again wondered how the
two of them had let a friendship as golden
as theirs fade away and die. Then without
warning a sharp pain sliced through her
stomach and she dropped to her knees.
"God, help me!"

She could hear Paul's voice, then he

helped her get to the hospital. Within an hour she was in emergency surgery. When she woke up, her entire family was in the room.

Tears in his eyes, her ten-year-old son, Skyler, took her hand. "I thought you were going to die, Mom."

"Everything's going to be fine, sweetheart."

"Promise?" Skyler looked doubtful.

Tracy smiled despite the tears in her eyes. "Promise."

But the next morning her doctor told them she had a tumor the size of a grapefruit in her abdomen. "Preliminary tests don't look good. If it's cancer, Tracy will need extensive surgery and chemotherapy. We should know more by tomorrow."

Tracy's immediate thought was her promise to Skyler. She was only thirty-eight. This couldn't be happening. Tracy and Paul held hands and asked God for a miracle.

"Take a nap," Paul told her. "God will work something out."

Tracy nodded. She was exhausted. She fell asleep praying, and almost immediately she began to dream she was calling out to God. Then, she heard God tell her what to do.

Have Anna come and pray.

176

When Tracy woke up, the words remained strong. But the idea was impossible. It had been five years of silence.

Tracy's thoughts drifted back to her freshman year of high school when she and Anna first became the very best of friends, sharing in every part of each other's lives. After college, they each married and settled only a few miles apart. They shared in each other's weddings and the births of each other's babies and the trials and triumphs of raising school-age children.

But then Anna had come to Tracy for a small loan. Their family van had given out, but with Anna's husband between jobs, borrowing money from a bank was not possible. Because of her friend's obvious need, Tracy checked with Paul and easily agreed to help. Anna promised payments once her husband, Ken, got a new job.

With the loan for five thousand dollars, Ken bought a van and got a new job that paid even better than the one he had lost. Finally, five months after the loan was made, Tracy and Paul invited Anna and Ken over for dinner. After a pleasant meal, Paul said, "You remember that loan. We were wondering if this would be a good time to set up a payment plan."

Anna and Ken exchanged a strange look.

She kept her eyes away from Tracy, focusing on only Paul. "What loan?"

The conversation turned stilted and tense. Ken denied knowing anything about the loan. Finally he snapped at Paul that yes, he would pay the money back, but their friendship would never be the same again. However, no payments came, only silence.

Eventually, Tracy and Paul agreed to forget about the loan and call it a gift, but it didn't matter. Weeks became months. Occasionally Tracy would call Anna, asking her out to lunch or over for coffee. But always Anna had an excuse. Nearly a year later, Anna told Tracy, "It's time to go our own ways."

Tracy was stunned and angry and filled with sorrow all at the same time. She and Anna had been closer than sisters, but it was all gone for reasons that made no sense.

That had been five years ago. So why now? *Lord, surely it's not you telling me to call her, right?*

Yes, daughter. Make the call. Anna needs to pray for you.

The thought seemed outrageous, but Tracy picked up the phone and dialed Anna's number from memory. Through choking tears, she said, "Anna, this is Tracy. I'm in the hospital and I'm sick, and . . . I think God wants me to ask you to come pray for me."

There was a long pause, then Anna said, "I'll be right there."

An hour later, Anna walked into the hospital room crying and said as the two hugged, "I'm sorry, Tracy, I didn't know what else to do. Ken left me a year ago." The announcement gave Tracy insight into the death of their friendship. After an hour's discussion, the air between them was clear once more.

"You wanted me to pray? What's wrong, Tracy?"

"I have a tumor the size of a grapefruit." She placed her hand over her abdomen. "They think it's cancer."

Anna nodded and placed her hand over Tracy's abdomen. "God, my dearest friend needs a miracle. Please remove the tumor from her body and make her well again." Anna's voice cracked. "You see, Lord, I've been sick in my heart over the loss of Tracy. And now I'm healed. So please, do the same thing for Tracy."

The two talked for another hour, then Anna left with promises to call the next day. "I believe tomorrow the doctors will find that a miracle has happened."

The next day, Paul arrived early. He was

stunned by the news of Anna's visit, the reconciliation, and the prayer.

But when the doctor came in, he said, "It looks like an aggressive cancer. We need to take more tests."

The blow was more than Tracy had imagined. She had clung to Anna's parting words — that God might work a miracle and heal her. Now, she felt she'd been handed a death sentence.

Tests were done that morning, and two hours later the doctor was back again. He entered the room with a strange look on his face and through Tracy's gown he carefully felt her abdomen. "It's gone."

"What do you mean?" Paul was stunned.

"The tests showed absolutely no signs of the tumor. I'm feeling the same place where the tumor was yesterday, but it's completely gone. Tumors that size don't just disappear." But additional tests reaffirmed it was true.

Tracy's heart swelled within her at the miracle God had given them. She went home to a welcome that included Anna and her children. When the two friends had a moment alone, Tracy thanked her for having the faith to pray for a miracle.

"We were both healed," Anna said. "You of your tumor and me of my guilt and shame." Her eyes shone. "God didn't give us one miracle, he gave us two."

His father was sick in bed, suffering from fever and dysentery. Paul went in to see him and, after prayer, placed his hands on him and healed him.

ACTS 28:8

WEEK 29.
To Run, to Fly

SCRIPTURE READING:
ECCLESIASTES 4:9–12

Delight yourself in the LORD and he will give you the desires of your heart.

PSALM 37:4

Steven Sanders and Jimmy Rowden grew up next door to each other as best buddies. Both boys were being raised in broken homes, in which their mothers were busy working two jobs. So not only did they do everything together, they needed each other.

Both boys dreamed high. Steven wanted to "be the best pilot in the world." Jimmy was the fastest boy in his class. He dreamed of becoming an Olympic runner. The trouble was that no one else thought their dreams were attainable, especially their mothers.

Nevertheless, Steven and Jimmy believed nothing could stop them from reaching their goals. Sometimes they'd run through a nearby field — Steven with his hands outstretched like wings, shouting, "I want to fly!" and Jimmy dashing as fast as the wind and shouting, "I want to run!"

But all that changed one summer day before fifth grade. Jimmy's dad took him swimming with his cousins to a lake that had a wooden platform in the middle of a roped-off swimming area. Jimmy and his three cousins started a game of tag on the platform. Always quicker than the others, Jimmy could not be caught. Finally ganging up on Jimmy, the three cousins rushed down the platform toward him.

Forgetting his father's warning, Jimmy dove into the shallow water to escape. The next second his head hit bottom and he felt a crushing, burning feeling in his spine. He couldn't kick, couldn't make himself rise to the surface, couldn't do anything.

People rushed to help him, and he was taken to a nearby hospital, but the doctors could do nothing to change the situation. Later that day, Jimmy received the worst news of his life. He was paralyzed from the waist down.

Steven didn't know something was wrong until two days later. Jimmy should've been home from his trip with his father, but Steven hadn't seen a sign of him or his mother. Finally he went to Jimmy's door and knocked. An old woman with red, swollen eyes answered the door.

"Is Jimmy home?"

"He's been hurt. I'm his grandma." She explained that Jimmy had broken his neck and was paralyzed from the waist down. Jimmy would never run again.

When Jimmy came home in a wheelchair, it took four days before Steven felt comfortable going to visit him. When he did, he wasn't sure what to say. Finally Jimmy broke the silence. "I still want to run."

Steven nodded. "I still want to fly."

Over the next few weeks, the two spent more of their free time together than apart. One day Steven wheeled Jimmy near the empty field and onto a stretch of dead-end roadway. This was where their dreams had always felt most possible. But now, they seemed dead.

Jimmy turned to Steven. "Think I'll ever run again?"

Even as a young boy, Steven knew better than to say yes, but he had a thought. "Let's have our dream now!"

Before Jimmy could say anything, Steven pushed the wheelchair faster and faster down the dead-end road. When he'd picked up enough speed, he hopped on the back of the wheelchair and let out a loud hoot. "I'm flying, Jimmy!"

When the wheelchair came to a stop, Steven walked around to the front of Jimmy's chair. "Now it's your turn." Then he stooped down, pulled Jimmy's limp legs around his own waist, and shouted, "Hold on!"

Jimmy looped his arms around Steven's neck.

With his friend balanced in piggy-back style, Steven took off running down the street, with Jimmy's laughter mixing with the wind. "I'm running again!"

In that moment their dreams felt as real as life itself.

But Jimmy did not learn to walk again. The friends began praying to God, asking him that one day Steven might learn to fly and Jimmy might run in the Olympics.

Their friendship came to a halt in seventh grade, when Jimmy and his mother moved to California. At first the boys wrote. But the letters eventually stopped.

Seventeen years passed, and Steven worked his way through the Air Force Academy and into a job as a commercial pilot. He often would thank God for letting his dream come true. But he wondered about Jimmy.

One morning as Steven made his way

routinely down the center aisle of his plane, he spotted a man who took his breath away. "Jimmy Rowden?"

The passenger's eyes grew wide. "Steven?"

"I can't believe it! I never thought I'd see you again."

"This is too strange. You got your dream, man! Look at you, flying this big ol' plane."

They talked about their families — both were married with two children — but all Steven could think about was whether Jimmy had gotten his dream. Then he spotted a pair of crutches lying next to Jimmy.

His old friend grabbed the crutches and swung himself up to his feet. He gave Steven a hard hug. "Did you pray for me?"

"Yes . . . all the time." Steven struggled to find his voice. Why hadn't God healed Jimmy? "I still do."

Jimmy smiled. "So God heard both our prayers. I'm flying to the qualifying meet for the Olympics, man!"

"The Olympics?"

"The Wheelchair Olympics! I'm a long shot for the hundred-yard! I was just remembering how we'd run that field shouting, 'I want to run!' "

"I want to fly."

"And here we are!" He gave Steven another hug.

Steven thought of the odds that he and Jimmy would reunite on the same plane, on the day Jimmy was headed to the Olympics. "It's a miracle, after all."

Steven and Jimmy remained in touch. Jimmy qualified for the Wheelchair Olympics. A few months later, Steven flew out to watch the race. Jimmy won the gold medal, and both friends realized again the power of having a dream and letting God make it come true.

Hope deferred makes the heart sick, but a longing fulfilled is a tree of life.
PROVERBS 13:12

WEEK 30.
BROUGHT TOGETHER
BY A MIRACLE
SCRIPTURE READING:
PSALM 72

He will defend the afflicted among the people and save the children of the needy.
PSALM 72:4

Angie Winters had one passion in her job as a social worker in Manhattan — to help lonely children find families. Every week brought new girls and boys into her life, kids desperate for a family — either through foster care or adoption. Her passion was personal. She was adopted as an infant, placed into a loving family with six other children. She viewed adoption as the most beautiful gift an adult could ever possibly give to a child.

Despite days when New York City was too busy, too confining, she had made a commitment to stay. Her caseload was full and the kids needed her. She would stay until God showed her she was to do otherwise.

One morning Angie arrived at work and found her supervisor talking with someone in the waiting area. With them was a beautiful little girl with brown eyes and curly dark brown hair. Angie moved closer to the child and dropped slowly to her knees. "Hi."

After a few seconds, the girl lifted her eyes and gave the smallest wave. Angie loved this part, connecting with a child who was probably at the lowest point of her life — alone and without anyone to care for her.

Angie uttered a silent prayer for the girl, then found out her name was Karli and she was nearly three years old. Angie's supervisor told her that both parents had been killed in a car accident the previous night. Karli had been in her car seat and had no injuries. Angie was assigned her case and told to check for relatives.

Angie breathed another prayer, that God would use her to bring hope and a new family to this precious child. She approached the girl and stooped down again. "Karli, come here, honey."

The child blinked twice, then held out her hand. As she came forward, Angie was seized by the strangest thought. What if she could take Karli home and be the mother she would need? The idea faded as quickly as it had come. Angie had promised herself that she wouldn't get personally involved at work. But something about this child had found an immediate pathway to the center of Angie's heart.

Angie learned that Karli had a single aunt named Amy who lived outside Denver. She called the woman and found out Amy was twenty-six. Her deceased sister had been eight years older, and the two hadn't talked in years. Amy didn't know until that phone call that she even had a niece.

"I'm all she has?" Shock sounded in Amy's voice.

"Yes," Angie answered. "I'd like to bring Karli for a visit as soon as possible."

"You can come anytime, but I can't promise anything. This is all so sudden. I'm engaged."

"Of course. I'd like to bring her to see you this weekend, if that works for you."

Angie felt a strange nervousness. Amy hadn't even known about Karli? How would Amy provide a loving home if family wasn't important to her? But she tucked her fears away and stuck with the mind-set she'd been trained to have. Anytime a child could be with a healthy, fit relative, the child would always be better off.

That night Karli stayed with her, then the following morning they shared breakfast and headed to the airport. By the time they were on the plane, Angie felt a connection with the girl that she normally resisted.

They were almost to Denver when Karli fell asleep. Angie used the time to pray. *God, work a miracle for Karli. She's lost so much. And if Amy doesn't want her, let it be clear.* She paused and waited. She felt the Lord's presence very close, as near as her next breath. *I feel something special for this one. So if Amy doesn't want her, let me be a part of Karli's life. Please, God.*

Even as she finished the prayer she felt a strange tingling along her spine. She'd never prayed that way for a child in her care. Whatever it was about Karli, it was different, and Angie had the strangest feeling that God was up to something unusual.

When Angie and Karli arrived at the house, Amy stepped outside and froze in her tracks. Angie looked at Amy and her head began to spin. She might as well have been looking into a mirror.

"Are you . . . are you Amy?"

"Yes." Her voice was filled with shock. "You look exactly like me. Were you adopted?"

Angie began to tremble. "Yes. As a baby."

"Really?" Amy gasped. "Me, too."

Angie was breathless, not sure what to say. She looked down at the child. "This is Karli."

"Okay, let's go inside and talk."

Over the next hour Angie learned the truth about the unimaginable. She and Amy were born on the same day, in the same town. Their birth mother — whom neither girl knew — must have had identical twins and given them up to separate families. As soon as they realized the truth, they embraced, caught between laughing and crying.

Finally Angie sat back in her chair and stared at her newfound sister. "So you're an aunt. Have you thought about that?"

"Have you?" A bit of laughter slipped out. It took a few seconds for Angie to get it

"If you're her aunt" — Angie grinned — "I'm her aunt, too. Because adopted families are families all the same. Miracle families."

"Exactly."

The plans came together quickly. Reconnected with the identical twin sister she hadn't known existed, Angie moved to Denver. There she is able to marvel at the miracle of her life and spend as much time with Karli as she wants. As for Karli, she's doing well in her new family, with her new forever mother, Amy.

O great and powerful God, whose name is the LORD Almighty, great are your pur-

poses and mighty are your deeds.
JEREMIAH 32:18

Week 31.
A Warning from Heaven

SCRIPTURE READING:
PSALM 29

Whether you turn to the right or to the left, your ears will hear a voice behind you, saying, "This is the way; walk in it."

ISAIAH 30:21

Laughter had always been the glue that held together the friendship between Donna West and Vicki Cutter. They met in first grade, and their mothers often told them, "You two are more like sisters than friends."

It was true. And never more so than the summer of their fifteenth year. The girls were excited about starting their sophomore year at a Phoenix high school close to their homes. Every day and nearly every night since school let out they'd been inseparable. And one of their favorite ways to spend the days was hanging out at Donna's aunt's house. Aunt Kerry was only twenty-four and married to a great guy. The couple lived just a block from Donna and their backyard

194

had one of the nicest pools in the neighbor-hood.

Besides that, there was something differ-ent about Kerry. She and her husband believed in God and even talked about him in everyday conversations — all the time.

On a July day as the girls walked toward Kerry's house, Donna said, "Whatever Aunt Kerry has got, I want it. I just don't know if I want it now."

Vicki thought about that for a moment. "What was it she told us about? Something about Young Life?"

"Right," replied Donna. "It's a club that meets at school. Maybe we should check it out this fall."

Kerry greeted them at the front door. "Hey, I was just going to the store. Why don't you come with me. We can swim when we get back."

Donna and Vicki looked at each other and shrugged. With Kerry any outing was bound to be fun. And funny. Kerry had a great sense of humor and appreciated the silliness that was the trademark of the girls' friend-ship.

On the way to the store, Vicki told a funny story about a baseball game the day before. "So we're sitting in the bleachers and the game's about half over when Donna stands up, walks over to the dugout, and nudges one of our friends through the fence and asks him about halftime."

"I thought we'd missed it," Donna's voice was half whine, half giggle. "No one ever told me baseball doesn't have a halftime."

Aunt Kerry laughed in the front seat, and Donna and Vicki barely paused before telling her another story. By the time they reached the store, the three of them were breathless from laughing so hard.

When Kerry pulled in and parked the car near the store, the girls decided to stay in the car and talk. "I'll be right back," Kerry had said.

Shortly after Kerry went into the store, Donna's eyes lit up. "Hey . . . let's play a trick on Aunt Kerry and make her really laugh."

Less than ten minutes passed before Kerry Miller left the store and headed for the car. Almost immediately she noticed something was wrong — the girls were gone. As she climbed into the car, she recalled the tricks they'd played on her before, which were usually funny, but this was definitely not funny. She peered out the side window, searching for any sign of them. "Donna! Vicki!" Kerry yelled and waited. "Girls . . .

I'm leaving. This isn't funny."

God, where are they? Panic began to rattle the windows of Kerry's heart. What if it wasn't a joke? What if something had happened to them? In that instant, she decided to head straight for the police station for help. If something had happened to them, the officers could begin the search quickly. And if not, when the girls saw her car leaving the area, they were bound to come running from wherever they were hiding.

Kerry started the car, revved the engine, and put the car into first gear to drive ahead. Then, just as Kerry moved her foot off the brake and onto the gas pedal, she heard a distinct voice from the back of the car.

"Back up!" The voice was deep, with an intensity and authority that was beyond doubting. "Go backward!" Without hesitating, Kerry backed up five feet. Then she saw the girls, crouched low and giggling, in front of the car. Nausea rushed over Kerry and she felt her body grow weak. If she had sped forward, she would have run them over and possibly killed them both.

Unaware of the danger, the girls came giggling and climbed inside. "Tricked you!" Donna said.

Kerry turned around and said, "That

wasn't funny, girls." She was silent the rest of the drive home, choosing not to tell the girls about what had nearly happened until they pulled in the driveway. Then she explained how she was going to pull forward.

"But a voice stopped me. An audible voice told me to back up instead."

"Wow." Donna felt more than a little guilty about what they'd done. "A real voice. But how can someone talk to you if no one's there?"

"Well . . . I'd say it was a miracle." Kerry turned around and for the first time explained her faith to the girls. "I have a relationship with God, not just a religion. Is that something you'd like to know more about?"

Both girls nodded their heads. And for the first time that summer, the story Kerry shared with them wasn't merely something to make them laugh. It was the truth about her faith in God and how Donna and Vicki could have the same faith.

Before the day was up, both girls made the most serious decision of their lives by praying with Kerry. Not just thanking God for the miraculous voice that saved their lives, but asking him to be in their lives the way he was in Aunt Kerry's.

Today, if you hear his voice, do not harden
your hearts.

HEBREWS 4:7

WEEK 32.
IN NEED OF A
FRIEND
SCRIPTURE READING:
1 SAMUEL 18:1–4

A man of many companions may come to ruin, but there is a friend who sticks closer than a brother.

PROVERBS 18:24

Bonner Davis knew the end was near. He had advancing throat cancer, mounting medical bills, and no way to pay for the experimental treatment that could save his life.

A retired forest ranger, Bonner and his wife, Angela, existed on his meager pension and a faith bigger than the Smoky Mountains. Once in a while, he would tell Angela that though he looked forward to heaven, he didn't want to leave her.

Angela's answer was always the same. "God knows what we need. Somehow he'll give us a miracle."

In nearby Spartanburg, millionaire Olsen Matthews was celebrating his sixtieth birthday. Without any family, he chose to spend his day in his small plane. He'd been in the air twenty minutes when some soul-searching took over. What was life about, anyway? He had great wealth, but no friends. And what if God was real? What if he wasn't right with God when he died? The possibility set his nerves on edge and made him wish once more for a friend who knew something about God.

Suddenly, Olsen heard a sharp pop and the engine cut out. He stayed calm, then flipped a series of switches to restart the motor, but none of them worked. Now his only hope was to glide the plane down and make an emergency landing. At the same time, the plane could catch a wrong current and plummet to the ground.

"God!" He called the name out loud. "If you're real, help me. I'm not ready to go."

Two minutes passed in textbook fashion, but then a strong current dropped a wing of the plane and the craft tumbled. Olsen had a thousand feet to go before hitting land, but then he spotted a lake. *That's my only hope.*

"Water, God! Lead me to the water."

As the ground rushed up to meet him, his plane suddenly fell to the left and hit the lake. There was the rush of cold wetness filling the cabin . . . then darkness.

Bonner saw the plane free-fall into the lake at the edge of his property. "Angela, quick! Call 911. A plane just crashed into the lake."

An outdoorsman, Bonner had always been in good shape. But the cancer and meds had taken a toll, and as he ran toward the lake he could barely catch his breath.

The situation was grim. One wing jutted out of the water, but the plane was otherwise buried in ten feet of water seventy-five yards offshore.

Bonner couldn't catch his breath, but whoever was in the plane was drowning. Bonner uttered a silent prayer, then dove in and swam as fast as he could. After five minutes, he reached the wing and though his lungs were burning, he took a deep breath and dove down. He tried twice to open the fuselage door, and finally on the third try, the door swung free.

Bonner was out of air. He swam to the surface, nauseated from the effort, grabbed another breath, and went back down. This time he found the pilot and felt around until he was sure the person was alone. Feeling as though he could black out at any second, Bonner dragged the unconscious man to the surface. Bonner was completely exhausted, and the pilot wasn't breathing.

Help me, God. Bonner replayed the words as he kept himself and the man afloat. Swimming with a strength that wasn't his own, Bonner dragged the pilot to shore. On the beach, despite his exhaustion he managed to administer CPR for three minutes until an emergency crew took over. He began to walk away but then collapsed to the ground.

Angela saw him drop. She called to the paramedics and explained about his cancer. "Help him, please."

An emergency worker moved quickly and hooked Bonner up to intravenous fluids. They took him to the hospital, and four hours later he went home. Before he left, he heard that the CPR had saved the pilot's life.

The next day the Davises received a visitor.

"My name's Olsen Matthews. You saved my life." The man shook Bonner's hand. "The paramedics said you were praying out loud, thanking God at the scene."

"My wife and I were both praying," Bonner said.

The man's eyes grew watery. "Thank you for that." He motioned toward their house. "Could I come in?"

The two men talked for almost an hour. Olsen explained that he'd heard from his doctors about Bonner's cancer. "I have a check for you. Maybe it'll help with your medical costs."

Then Olsen asked Bonner about God. With Angela at his side, Bonner told him about their faith. At the end of the conversation, Olsen and Bonner prayed.

"Could you be my friend, Bonner? Someone I could visit now and then, someone to talk to about God?"

A smile lifted the corners of Bonner's mouth. "Definitely."

"Good." Olsen stood to leave. "I was asking God about a friend when I crashed. And now he's worked everything out . . . for me and you."

When the man was gone, Bonner opened the check and fell silent. The check was for one million dollars. In the note section it read, "Use this to get better."

Bonner did just that, using the money for the costly experimental treatment. Three years later, in one of their many times together, Bonner and Olsen agreed that God had done more than take part in the miracle of Olsen's rescue and Bonner's healing.

He also gave them the miracle of new friendship.

A friend loves at all times, and a brother is born for adversity.

PROVERBS 17:17

WEEK 33.
TWICE THE MIRACLE

SCRIPTURE READING:
EXODUS 2:1–10

Sons are a heritage from the LORD, children a reward from him.

PSALM 127:3

Bob and Sarah Williams married with one thought in mind: Children were out of the question. Track stars at the University of Illinois, Bob and Sarah saw life as a continuous athletic event. They moved to the Pacific Northwest and took jobs with Nike. Spare time was spent jogging, playing tennis, and working out. Because of that, life came to a complete standstill when Sarah returned from the doctor one day, still in shock. Despite their efforts to the contrary, she was pregnant.

Sarah's mother — a woman of strong faith — visited and prayed for her. "God has a plan for this child. Otherwise you wouldn't be pregnant. Don't think of all you've lost because of this; think of all that lies ahead."

Sarah had never prayed much, but faced

with serious decisions regarding their future and the future of the child, she had nowhere else to turn. "God, if you're there, what're we supposed to do?"

Bob, too, found himself praying. "The way I see it, the fact that Sarah got pregnant is a miracle. Now, God, show us whether we should keep this child."

Sarah was in bed still mulling over the possibilities when she felt the faintest stirrings in her abdomen — like butterfly wings against the underneath side of her tummy. It was her baby!

"Wake up, Bob. You won't believe this."

Bob opened his eyes and looked at the alarm clock. "It's midnight. Can't it wait?"

"No. I felt the baby, Bob! I really did."

"You mean . . . you felt it move?"

"Yes! Like butterfly wings on the inside of me."

Sarah's enthusiasm was contagious, and by the time she was six months pregnant, she and Bob were looking forward to being parents. That week they went to the doctor's office and found out the biggest news of all: Sarah was carrying twin boys.

Joy and disbelief surrounded Bob and Sarah. Life would be so exciting having twin sons. All that weekend they shopped, setting up the spare bedroom as a nursery complete with matching cribs and a sports theme.

But on Sunday night Sarah was seized by sharp pains in her midsection. By eleven o'clock, Sarah was doubled over. Worse, she had started bleeding. Doctors at the hospital confirmed Sarah's fears. Her placenta had torn and she was bleeding. The babies were having some sort of trouble, and surgery was imminent.

As Sarah tried to listen to the doctor, she felt herself drifting in a way she was helpless to control. When she woke up nearly two days later, she didn't have to ask what had happened. Her abdomen was smaller and Bob was crying. The babies had not survived.

The grieving process was worse than anything Sarah could have imagined. She never saw her boys, never got to hold them. Worse, well-meaning friends would on occasion say that maybe Bob and Sarah weren't meant to have kids after all.

As the months passed Sarah learned that her uterus had been too damaged for her to have more children. But they were no longer content to live the remainder of their lives without children. Finally, a year after the loss of their twin boys, they began adoption proceedings. Months were needed for a home study and appointments with a social worker. They took evening courses about children at risk and parental bonding. The nine-month mark came, and still no babies.

After losing their boys Bob and Sarah had stopped praying, not sure of a God who could let their babies die. But they began again after Sarah's mother explained, "God doesn't make mistakes. He said there'd be trouble in this world, and there is. But he still asks us to pray."

Then one day they received a call from their social worker. "I've got a little boy for you."

Sarah's heart soared. God was giving them a son, a child to ease the place in her heart where her twins had taken root. "How old is he?"

"Well — he's not exactly born yet. But if you can get to the hospital in the next hour, you'll probably be there in time for the delivery."

The woman went on to explain that the mother had lived on the streets until a week earlier. A call to her social worker assured her that they would help her find a loving family to adopt her baby.

Bob and Sarah grabbed a blanket and an infant layette, one they'd purchased back before their babies died. They arrived at the hospital and an hour later a doctor appeared in the waiting room.

"The delivery went beautifully. Mother and babies are doing very well."

Bob gazed at the doctor. "Babies? I'm sorry; maybe you have the wrong couple."

"You're Bob and Sarah Williams, right?"

"Right, but . . ."

"The mother realized she was carrying twins."

At that instant, the social worker entered the waiting room. There were tears in her eyes. "You're approved for more than one child. The babies are both boys. If you're willing to take them, they'll belong to you."

Sarah's knees shook and she grabbed Bob's elbow to keep from falling. Twin boys who needed a home? Their nursery was still the way it had been set up — two cribs, twin dressers, all of it ready for two twin boys.

Bob put his arm around Sarah. "It's the miracle we've been praying for."

And so it was. Bob and Sarah were convinced that the delay had been part of God's plan. For only he could have arranged for twin baby boys to help fill the emptiness left by the infants they'd lost.

No eye has seen, no ear has heard, no mind has conceived what God has prepared for those who love him.

WEEK 34.
ANGEL IN A PICKUP
SCRIPTURE READING:
GENESIS 16:7–14

While Peter was still thinking about the vision, the Spirit said to him, "Simon, three men are looking for you. So get up and go downstairs. Do not hesitate to go with them, for I have sent them."

ACTS 10:19–20

The two doctors had been best friends and partners for twenty years. William Sutter and Harry Bateman were such "kindred spirits," they often joked that even their wives could barely tell them apart.

The two men found land in a remote canyon outside Cottonwood, Arizona, bought nearby properties, and moved their families out into the desert. The drive was long and winding, but the friends found the extra effort worth it.

One night in late August, Harry and his wife were watching a movie at a theater in Sedona when Harry was seized by a strange thought. *Will is in trouble;* he was sure of it.

About that time, thunder sounded above the movie and he jerked in his seat.

"Why so jumpy?" his wife whispered.

"Will's in trouble. I have a feeling. Let's go."

Twenty-one miles away, Will had been on his way home. As he turned onto the canyon road that led to his house, a monsoon unlike any he'd ever seen let loose. Canyon signs warned of landslides and flash floods, but neither had happened in ten years. Now, though, rain was coming in sheets, and it looked as if the earth along the hillside had given way.

Suddenly a pickup approached. As it neared, it halted and flashed its lights. Will stopped and rolled his window down to see the driver, a white-haired man with light eyes that almost glowed.

"Can't get through!" the man shouted. "Part of the road's gone."

Will had a sinking feeling in his gut. He had to get home. Besides, the road couldn't be that bad. "Thanks," he yelled. "I'll take my chances."

The man looked hard at him. Will looked away and hit the gas pedal. *Strange guy. What was he doing out here, anyway? Never seen him before.*

Will went slower with each turn. Suddenly, without warning, a wall of water and mud crashed against his Suburban and pushed it toward the edge of the canyon. The drop was more than two hundred feet and Will could do nothing to stop his vehicle.

"God! Help me!" Will shouted the words. He had a few seconds before going over the edge.

Then, suddenly, his Suburban jolted to a stop.

Will looked out his window and saw that the water was still flowing against his car, but not as strongly as before. Every few seconds he could feel his front tires slip a little, but still his vehicle held. When the flow stopped, he tried to open his door, but the movement of his body caused his Suburban to lurch a few feet closer to the edge. *Okay, God. Give me a miracle, please. Get me out of this.*

Outside the theater, Harry and his wife climbed into their Explorer as a pickup pulled up. Harry was trembling now, desperately worried about Will. He rolled down his window and looked at the man. His hair was bright white, and his eyes held an unnatural light, otherworldly. "Can I help you?"

"Do you have a winch?" the man asked. "There's a guy off Old Canyon Highway stuck in the mud. He's gonna need a winch."

Old Canyon Highway was their road. "I'm headed that way; I'll see what I can do."

The entire drive, the feeling that Will was in danger only grew stronger for Harry.

"Do you think maybe this is a little crazy?" Harry's wife asked. "Will is home tonight."

"I don't care. I've never felt like this in my life. He's in trouble, and God wants me to help him."

They kept driving through sections of the road that were nearly buried in mud. The rain had stopped, but the damage was everywhere. "Flash floods," he told his wife. "That must be what that guy was talking about."

One more turn and Harry's breath caught in his throat. There was Will's vehicle, the headlights flashing. It had slid sideways off the road toward the canyon's edge, and though a bank of mud remained wedged against the driver's door, a tree stump on the passenger side kept the Suburban from going over.

Harry stopped. "Will! Are you in there?"

"Yes!" Will's voice was shaken. "Stay there. I'm not stable. One wrong move and —"

At that instant, the car slid another few inches.

"I've got a winch. Hold on!" As Harry said the words, he wondered how the man in the pickup had driven from the remote canyon where Will was stuck to the theater parking lot in search of someone with a winch, but he had no time to analyze it. Cell phones didn't work out here, so a rescue would be up to him.

Moving as fast as possible, he found his winch and, using a nearby tree for support, braced the Suburban in six places. Just as he attached the last rope, the Suburban pulled away from the tree stump and slid freely toward the edge of the canyon. But Harry's ropes held, and the vehicle stopped a few feet short of going over.

"Praise God!" Will shouted as he climbed out of the Suburban and made his way to Harry's car.

There the two men compared notes and realized they'd both had an encounter with the man in the pickup who had white hair and glowing eyes.

"Do you think maybe . . . ," Harry's wife said. "Could he have been an angel?"

For a long moment no one said anything. They didn't have to, really. God in his miraculous wonder had said enough for all of them.

We will not fear, though the earth give way and the mountains fall into the heart of the sea, though its waters roar and foam and the mountains quake with their surging.
PSALM 46:2–3

Week 35.
In the Nick of Time
SCRIPTURE READING:
GENESIS 19:12–29

I will save you; you will not fall by the sword but will escape with your life, because you trust in me, declares the LORD.
JEREMIAH 39:18

As Taylor Evans climbed the thirty-foot utility pole with a damaged light fixture, two thoughts occurred to him. First, he hadn't heard from his best friend, Aaron, in six months. And second, he no longer expected to.

He glanced at the storm clouds overhead and whispered a familiar prayer. *Get me down safely, God.*

As he continued his climb, images of Aaron came once more to his mind. They'd been closer than brothers in high school and played football and basketball together. Aaron had been good enough to win a football scholarship, but his grades were too low. So they both went to community college, where they could both play football and Aaron could hope for a scholarship.

The first season was going great until Aaron took a full-force blow to his knee and collapsed to the ground. His knee was destroyed. Several operations and a long rehabilitation followed, but his football days were over.

That was the beginning of the end, Taylor thought as he kept climbing the utility pole. He'd prayed for Aaron for years since then, rescued him when he was stone-drunk, taken him to counseling centers for his depression, and most of all told him about God.

But Aaron didn't want to hear about answers. Instead he grew more distant from Taylor every year. Finally, that past spring, Aaron said, "Leave me alone, Taylor. We're finished." It appeared that his best friend was finally and completely out of his life.

Aaron Grant walked out of church and realized he had let losing football nearly cost him his soul.

Two months earlier, Aaron had been at a bar when his old coach approached him and asked how he was. Aaron was too drunk to respond coherently. The man who'd dreamed with him and believed in him had shrugged and walked away in disgust.

Aaron hit rock bottom. The next day he was seized with remorse for the way he'd treated his best friend. Hadn't Taylor always been there? Hadn't Taylor forced him through his rehab and run with him?

Aaron made a decision to change. He would get his act together, find out about this God that Taylor talked about so often, and walk away from alcohol altogether. Then, in a few months, he'd call Taylor and thank him for being the best friend anyone could ever have.

The next two months passed in a blur of intensity. He sought counseling for his depression and alcohol abuse and took a job working at the local supermarket. At night he started his college classes up again, and three times a week he attended church and Bible studies.

That afternoon, with storm clouds building overhead, Aaron knew it was time. As he drove across town, he was ten minutes from calling Taylor and making everything right again. He could hardly wait.

Perched at the top of the utility pole, Taylor knew the protocol: get down immediately in the case of an electrical storm. But he knew he had ten minutes at least, maybe fifteen. He wouldn't be stupid.

He opened the glass fixture and saw the frayed wires. Taylor went right to work, all the while keeping one eye on the storm. *Just three minutes, God.*

At that instant his cell phone rang. His phone had one ring for personal calls and one with short staccato beeps for work emergencies. This ring was short staccato beeps. He thought about ignoring the call, but someone could be trapped or injured on a job site. He flipped his phone and barked a short hello.

Only a few garbled words sounded on the other end. His frustration doubled. This happened once in a while when the utility pole interfered with phone reception.

He began the arduous climb back down the pole. When he reached the bottom, he slipped inside his car to make the call. At that exact moment, Taylor felt the hair on the back of his neck stand straight up. Before he could blink, a bolt of lightning zapped the utility pole, slicing across the very spot where he had been working.

Seconds passed as Taylor stared at the smoking tip of the utility pole. He would have been dead instantly. Finally, as the shock began to wear off, Taylor closed his eyes. *God, you saved me from certain death. Thank you . . . and thank you for whoever —*

He hadn't answered the emergency message. He checked the caller's phone number, pressed the Send button, and waited.

On the third ring, Aaron Grant answered. "Hello?"

"Aaron?" Taylor's mind was reeling.

"Taylor, you won't believe it. I've changed. I had to call you and tell you so myself."

Taylor gave a light shake of his head and tried to clear the cobwebs. Something wasn't making sense here. "Did you call me on my emergency line?"

"No. Just your normal cell phone number."

"That's impossible." Slowly the pieces fell into place. The ring had come through as an emergency by some God-directed miracle. How appropriate that God would use Aaron this way. "You know something, Aaron? I think you just saved my life."

"No, man, that's not it. I'm calling to thank you for saving mine. Hoping you'll forgive me."

"Tell you what." Taylor slipped his keys into the ignition. "Let's meet at the diner by the community college. You aren't going to believe what just happened."

Do you know how God controls the clouds and makes his lightning flash?

JOB 37:15

WEEK 36.
TAKE IT TO GOD

SCRIPTURE READING:
2 KINGS 5:1–14

The wolf will live with the lamb, the leopard will lie down with the goat, the calf and the lion and the yearling together; and a little child will lead them.

ISAIAH 11:6

Kathy Hester had been looking forward to the mountain campout on Labor Day weekend, but her hectic schedule had her frazzled the morning of the trip. She said to her husband, "I keep reminding myself this is supposed to be fun."

Jason nodded. "Sometimes it's all what we make of things."

In less than a minute Kathy could hear him singing and encouraging the children to get their things packed. *Why is he so happy?* she thought.

An hour later they were on the road and Jason tried to lighten her mood. "Looks like great weather."

Kathy felt tears stinging her eyes. "Inside

224

my heart there's nothing but storm clouds. All I want to do is ask God to help me see the sunshine again."

"Well" — Jason grinned — "then ask him."

"No." Kathy stared out the window. "He isn't concerned about my vacation."

Four hours later they pulled into their campsite high up in the White Mountains of central Arizona. The kids and Jason chattered merrily, but the sky had clouded up. It was five o'clock before the camp was set up.

"How 'bout a little fishing?" Jason suggested, followed by hoots of approval from the three children.

"Sure." Kathy forced a smile.

The evening was pleasant, filled with laughter and easy conversation. But by the time they got back to camp, the sky was ominous-looking. An hour later lightning flashed angrily across the sky, thunder cracked, and rain poured onto their camp.

"Jason," Kathy whispered. "We need to find some shelter."

Jason rolled over on his cot. "Honey, the tent's waterproof. Everything'll be fine."

"We can't stay under the trees with the lightning."

"Kathy, storms roll through here nearly

225

every night in the summer. Get some sleep."

She peered anxiously through the flap. Just then five-year-old Megan's head peeked up from her sleeping bag. "Mommy, if you're afraid, why don't you pray?"

Kathy reached out and patted Megan's blonde hair. "Yes, honey, that's a good idea." In truth, she thought it was too small a matter to bother God about.

In the morning, the rain had stopped but the sky was gloomy gray, darkening even Jason's mood as they began preparing breakfast on the wet picnic table. After breakfast the Hesters headed for a nearby stream. As they fished the thunder and lightning returned and rain fell harder than before. Heading back to the camp, a ranger told them, "We're in for steady rain all day."

"Fun vacation," Kathy mumbled.

The rain fell for three hours while they stayed in the tent playing games and trying to stay warm. Finally, Jason stuck his hand outside the tent. "The rain's let up a little. Let's get a fire started so we can dry out."

Jason and Kathy worked feverishly trying to ignite the damp wood with newspaper. But after an hour, the couple had created only a great deal of smoke and even more frustration. They even tried holding an umbrella over the wood. Another hour of futile attempts passed.

During that time, Megan and their seven-year-old son, Luke, slipped out of the tent and began watching.

"Without a fire, we can forget dinner," Kathy said.

Luke and Megan glanced at each other and then Luke motioned for her to follow him.

"Where are you going?" Kathy asked.

"We have to do something," Luke said. "We'll be right back."

Kathy nodded. "All right. Don't go too far."

"We won't." Megan smiled. Five minutes later they returned and sat nearby, grinning and glancing upward.

At about that time, the rain stopped. Not long afterward, the fire pit was blazing and the Hesters gathered around to dry out. Suddenly Kathy remembered the children's brief disappearance.

"Megan, why did you go off into the woods?"

The girl smiled sweetly. "Well, we didn't want to starve. Luke said we should ask God to stop the rain."

A sinking feeling settled over Kathy's stomach. It had happened again. Two adults, both strong in their faith in God and the power of prayer, who'd done everything except pray — the one thing their young children had chosen to do.

"He heard us, Mommy," Megan said matter-of-factly. "You and Daddy always say if you have a problem, take it to God in prayer. Right?"

Kathy thought of her gloomy mood and how she'd considered her problems too insignificant for God. "It sure is, Megan. Thanks for helping me remember."

Despite the gray sky, no rain fell on the campsite until after nine o'clock that evening. The rain continued through the night and let up only long enough for them to pack their camping gear for the trip back home. On the way out, they asked the ranger about the rain.

"Never let up all day yesterday," the ranger said.

Kathy glanced at Jason. "We had about five hours without rain in the early evening."

The ranger scratched his head. "Why, that's the craziest thing. I was only a few hundred yards away and I didn't get a bit of relief all evening."

As they drove away, Kathy told Jason about Megan and Luke's prayer that the rain would stop. Jason laughed. "See . . . no prayer is too small for God."

"I guess you're right." Kathy grinned. God did indeed care about the small details after all.

Pray continually.

1 THESSALONIANS 5:17

Week 37.
On Angels' Wings

SCRIPTURE READING:
DANIEL 6

The LORD is near to all who call on him, to all who call on him in truth. He fulfills the desires of those who fear him; he hears their cry and saves them.

PSALM 145:18–19

Jackie Connover had driven the dangerous road a hundred times. She and her husband, Michael, had spent the past seven years as counselors for Mountaintop Christian Camp, a retreat-like cluster of cabins nestled high in the mountains above Colorado Springs. The two-lane highway from the city below to the camp was barely etched into the side of the mountain and bordered by sheer drops of several hundred feet.

On the afternoon of August 10, Jackie buckled her only son, Cody, into his car seat, checking to be sure it was attached securely to the backseat of their brand-new Ford Ranger. Jackie had loaded supplies in the back of her vehicle, and as they drove back up the mountainside she felt the supplies shifting. She slowed down, knowing that a spill could trigger a dangerous accident.

Glancing in her rearview mirror, she saw several impatient drivers behind her, but it was too dangerous for her to accelerate and there were no turnouts and only inches separated the road from the canyon's edge. *Help me, God. Protect us, please.*

Worried that one of the drivers might try to pass — a common cause of serious accidents along the highway — Jackie directed the truck onto a narrow shoulder and slowly applied the brakes. The other cars quickly passed and Jackie sighed aloud. Then, without warning, the earth under the truck's right tire gave way and in an instant the Ranger began tumbling down the mountainside into the canyon.

"Hold on!" Jackie screamed, hearing Cody cry. The Ranger tumbled wildly downward and Jackie was slammed with remarkable force against the shoulder harness of her seat belt and then against the truck's shell with each complete roll. *I'm going to die,* she thought.

"Cody!" She screamed but heard nothing.

Finally, more than five hundred feet down the mountain, the Ranger came to rest upside down. Jackie was conscious but trapped in the front seat. A warm liquid was oozing around her eyes, mouth, and ears.

"Cody!" she shouted, desperately working herself out of the mangled Ranger. It was then that she saw Cody's car seat still strapped to the backseat, its body harness still snapped in place. But Cody was gone.

"Cody!" Tears streamed down her battered face as she gazed up the steep hillside for any sign of him. Then she fell to her knees and asked God to help her find him.

Suddenly, she saw people standing along the road's edge waving toward her. "Are you okay?" a man yelled.

"Yes! But I can't find my son!"

Jackie began making her way up the hillside. She was coughing up blood, and her head felt ready to explode. Still she continued to call Cody's name. Finally, when she was forty feet from the road, she heard his voice. "Mommy! Mommy!" he cried. "I'm here!"

At that moment three bystanders scrambled down the cliff toward a small clearing hidden from the road and reached the child at about the same time Jackie did.

Cody was sitting cross-legged on top of a soft, fern-fronded bush. His eyes were black and blue and he had dark purple bruises around his neck. His tiny body shook with fear and he was sobbing.

"Dear God, help us!" Jackie prayed out loud.

At about that time a medical helicopter landed on the highway. Paramedics surrounded Jackie and Cody and within minutes mother and son were strapped to straight boards and airlifted to Huntington Memorial Hospital.

Jackie's head had swollen to nearly twice its normal size. Her lungs were also badly damaged from the pressure of her life-saving seat belt. She was placed in intensive care and given a slim chance of survival.

Meanwhile, doctors determined that despite Cody's severely bruised neck there was no damage to his spinal column and no internal injuries.

When Michael reached Jackie's side several hours later, she was unconscious and so swollen and bruised he hardly recognized her. He prayed intently that she would survive, then went to find Cody.

The little boy began crying when Michael hurried in. As Cody described what had happened, he said, "Then I was on the bush but Mommy kept rolling and rolling."

"How did you wind up on the bush, honey?"

Cody wiped at his tears. "The angels took me out of the truck and set me down there. Right on the bush so I wouldn't be hurt. They were nice."

Suddenly a chill ran the length of Michael's spine.

"Do you know my angels, Daddy?"

Michael shook his head. "No, Cody, but they did a good job getting you out of the truck."

Over the next few days, as Jackie's condition improved, sheriff's investigators found the Ranger's back window in one piece a few yards down the mountain from the highway. They determined that in a matter of seconds, as the truck made its first roll, the back window popped out, and Cody somehow slipped through the straps of his seat belt and fell backward through the opening onto the soft bush.

"A virtual impossibility," the investigators said. "We will never know how Cody survived."

For Cody, the explanation was obvious.

Months later, as the family prepared their cabin for Christmas, Cody approached Jackie with a tree ornament shaped like an angel and said, "Angels don't really look like this. They look like nice daddies, but they're angels. Because that's what they said they were."

Left with no other explanation, she and her husband believe their son is telling the truth.

He will command his angels concerning you to guard you in all your ways; they will lift you up in their hands, so that you will not strike your foot against a stone.

PSALM 91:11–12

WEEK 38.
ANGEL IN THE NIGHT
SCRIPTURE READING:
DANIEL 8:15–27

Call to me and I will answer you and tell you great and unsearchable things you do not know.

JEREMIAH 33:3

Attractive and athletic, Julie and Bryan Foster lived a charmed life. They were in their twenties, shared a passion for country music and the outdoors, and loved each other's company.

Then Bryan got sick and sicker. Finally, he was diagnosed with acute lymphoblastic leukemia, the deadliest form of cancer. During the next three months, Bryan's cancer slipped into remission and he stayed the picture of health at six feet two inches and two hundred pounds.

Doctors discovered that Bryan's brother was a perfect match for a bone marrow transplant. But before the operation could be scheduled, Bryan's remission ended dramatically and he became too weak to undergo a transplant.

The doctor recommended that Bryan be admitted to Nashville's Vanderbilt Medical Center for continuous treatment in hopes of forcing the disease into remission. Bryan and Julie took medical leaves of absence from their jobs and moved into the hospital. Julie slept on a cot beside Bryan during his intensive chemotherapy and radiation treatments.

"You're going to be fine," Julie told Bryan.

Surrounded by other dying patients in the cancer ward, Bryan spent a great deal of time in prayer, asking God to take care of Julie no matter what happened to him. He prayed for remission but also asked God for the strength to accept his death if it was his time.

Months passed and his doctors gave up hope that Bryan's cancer would go into remission. A year after his original diagnosis, he weighed only one hundred pounds, was unable to walk, and rarely found the energy needed to sit up in bed.

"I don't think he has much longer, Julie," one doctor said. "I want you to be ready."

Julie nodded, tears streaming down her cheeks. But she was not ready to say good-bye to the only man she'd ever loved.

Then in the middle of the night, she was

awakened by a nurse. "Mrs. Foster! Your husband has gone."

Thinking that Bryan had died, Julie sat straight up. His bed was empty. "Where did you take him?"

"We haven't moved him. We came in to check his vital signs and he was gone."

"He hasn't walked in two months. Besides, someone would have seen him."

As Julie ran from the room toward the elevators, her eyes caught a movement in the chapel. Heading for the door and peering inside, she was stunned to see Bryan sitting in one of the pews, talking with a white-haired man she'd never seen before. Anger worked its way through Julie's insides. Why had Bryan left without saying anything? And who was this man? Where had he come from at three in the morning?

After several minutes passed, she walked into the chapel. The stranger was dressed in a red-checked flannel shirt, blue jeans, and work boots. His skin was so white it appeared transparent.

"Bryan? Where have you been?"

He looked up and smiled, appearing stronger than he had in months. "Hi, honey. I'll be back in the room soon."

Julie turned toward the stranger and he looked at her. She was struck by the brilliance of his clear blue eyes.

Who is he? she wondered. "What's going on?"

"Julie, please." Bryan's voice was gentle but adamant. "I'll be back in the room soon!"

Reluctantly, Julie returned to his room and waited until finally Bryan joined her. Julie almost didn't recognize him. With a wide grin on his face, Bryan was full of energy and walked with a strength that simply wasn't possible. He was obviously at peace.

"Okay, who was he? What happened?"

"Julie, he was an angel."

Bryan's words were so confident they left no doubt in Julie's mind that he believed what he said. She was silent a moment.

"I believe you," she said softly. "Tell me about it."

Bryan said he had suddenly awakened and experienced an overpowering urge to go to the chapel. His intravenous tubing had already been removed (which none of the nurses remembered doing when asked later). Climbing out of bed, he was suddenly able to move without any weakness. When he got to the chapel, he knelt to pray and then heard a voice.

"Are you Bryan Foster?"

"Yes." Bryan turned around and the man was there.

"Do you need forgiveness for anything?"

For years Bryan had held bitter feelings toward a relative. Slowly, he told the man of his hatred.

The man told Bryan that God had forgiven him. "What else is bothering you?"

"Julie. My wife," Bryan said. "I'm worried about what's going to happen to her."

The man smiled peacefully. "She will be fine." Then he knelt alongside Bryan and the two men prayed together. Finally, the man said to Bryan, "Your prayers have been answered. You can go now."

Bryan was certain the man was an angel.

Julie desperately wanted to talk to the man herself. She ran back to the chapel but he was gone. Next, she checked the guards posted at each elevator as well as those at the hospital's main entrance. No one had seen anyone who fit the man's description. Feeling defeated, she returned to Bryan's room.

"Didn't find him, right?" Bryan said, grinning.

"Where did he go? I really want to talk to him."

"I guess he went to wherever he came from, honey."

Slowly, Julie understood. If he was an angel, of course he'd disappeared. Bryan was right.

The next day Bryan was full of energy. Many physical manifestations of his illness seemed to have lessened or disappeared. Both Julie and Bryan thought he was miraculously in remission. Bryan spent much of the day encouraging and praying with other patients.

Two days later Julie awoke with a premonition of Bryan's death, which made no sense. He looked vibrant and strong. And if his prayers had been answered, he was on his way to recovery.

That afternoon, Bryan suffered a pulmonary hemorrhage and immediately dozens of medical personnel swarmed around. While the doctors tried to save his life, Julie collapsed to the floor and began to pray. Almost instantly, she felt a peace wash over her and realized that this was part of God's plan. Bryan had prayed that she would be all right, and in that instant she knew she would be. No matter what happened.

"Julie!" Bryan's voice was clear, calm. Julie jumped to her feet and took her husband's hand.

"It's okay, honey," she whispered, her tear-covered face gazing down at him. "It's okay."

Two minutes later Bryan was dead.

Now, well over ten years later, Julie believes that Bryan's prayers were answered that night. He was given the gift of peace, of accepting his fate and not fighting it in fear. Also, he had been released from the bondage of bitterness and graced with God's forgiveness. And he had been given assurance that Julie would survive without him. An assurance she clings to still.

Peace I leave with you; my peace I give you. I do not give to you as the world gives. Do not let your hearts be troubled and do not be afraid.

JOHN 14:27

Week 39.
The Sweetest Friend

SCRIPTURE READING:
PSALM 46

Arise, cry out in the night, as the watches of the night begin; pour out your heart like water in the presence of the Lord.

LAMENTATIONS 2:19

Tami Bolton's father needed just two words to turn her entire life upside down. "We're moving!" he announced one day. Then he went on to explain that he'd found a job in Southern California where he could concentrate on his career in solar energy.

For a year Tami had known this day might come. But at sixteen she wasn't ready to leave Missouri, especially to be two thousand miles away from her married sister and friends.

"I can't move." Tears welled up in her eyes. "Everyone is here, Daddy. Can't you wait another year? Until I'm ready to live on my own?"

This was the job her father had been waiting years to get, and there was no changing

243

it. But that did not diminish the pain. Nothing would be the same in California. She'd miss all the milestones she and her friends had planned on — prom, graduation, college — as well as her relationship with her older sister, Mari.

When she finally got a grip on her emotions, Tami said to her mother, "At least I'll have you and Misty."

Her mom's body stiffened at the mention of Tami's cat. "Honey, there's no way we can bring her. We'll be in a rented apartment without space to hunt. It's not fair to her. Mari has offered to take her. Try to understand."

Tami spent an hour crying in her room. She couldn't understand any of it. But she had no choice but to give in, even as she felt her world crumbling around her.

When they arrived in California, the Boltons found a small two-bedroom apartment. Although Tami tried to have a positive attitude, as the weeks passed she grew more homesick. She couldn't shake the feeling of isolation. Even after two months, when her parents bought a beautiful home with a swimming pool, that didn't help. Worst of all, she felt far from God, as if he were unaware of her broken heart.

A month later, Tami apologized to her parents for her sadness. "I'm happy for you. Really. It's just that I feel so lonely it's almost like I'm suffocating."

Two weeks later, on Tami's birthday, her parents presented her with a tiny gray kitten. For the first time since the move, she looked genuinely happy.

"Oh my goodness!" Tami squealed, taking the tiny kitten in her arms. "She's perfect. Thank you so much!"

Tami named the kitten Chloe, and with a new friend to keep her company, her outlook changed overnight. She began meeting more kids at school and enjoying her classes, and over the next few months, she spent hours playing with Chloe and teaching her the house rules.

Because Chloe was primarily an indoor cat, the Boltons had her declawed. After that, they were careful to not let her jump the fence around their house, because without her claws she had no way to defend herself. If she tried the fence, the neighbors' dogs chased her back.

Words could never express how thankful Tami was for Chloe. Many nights as Tami drifted off to sleep she would whisper a special thank-you to God for using the precious kitten to lift the dark clouds from her life.

Then one morning Tami lost track of Chloe, and the kitten disappeared. Frightened, Tami contacted the neighbors, but none had seen Chloe. Tami told herself the kitten would return within a few hours when she got hungry, but by evening she had not returned. Tami and her parents searched the neighborhood for hours. Two days passed, and Tami continued to search and call for her kitten after school.

By the third afternoon, Tami was losing hope as she walked home from the bus stop. A trickle of tears splashed the ground beneath her. How could this happen? Why? *Lord, you let me find a friend and now you've let her disappear. Couldn't you bring Chloe back to me? Please.*

But the truth was clearer than Tami wanted to admit. The chances that Chloe would come back now were almost non-existent. Either something had happened to the kitty or she'd been taken by someone.

Stepping into her backyard, Tami yelled, "Chloe. Here, Chloe." As she waited, she was finally overwhelmed with fear and loneliness. She turned toward the house and ran into her bedroom. There, she threw herself on her bed and began to yell.

"God, I can't handle this! I'm so lonely and Chloe was all I had. Now's she's gone, too. It's too much."

She continued until her anger and sobs were spent. Then she remembered that the Lord is close to the brokenhearted. Suddenly, Tami felt God's presence. The chasm that had developed between her and God disappeared in an instant. *You're my friend, too; right, God? Is that what you're trying to tell me?* A surge of hope swelled up within her. Yes, that was it. God was her friend, now and always. A friend better than Chloe.

Tami looked up and whispered, "Please, Lord, hear me now. I only need you. But I really want my cat to come home. I'm going out into the backyard, and I'm asking you to bring Chloe to me, if it is your will."

She felt that her request was childish, but she trusted with all her heart that God could hear her. She walked back out of the house, and there, sitting by the pool, was Chloe. She glanced at Tami casually as if she'd been there the whole time.

"Meow," she squeaked, then scampered toward Tami.

Tami fell on her knees, bowing her head in thanks. Not because her cat was back, but because she had rediscovered a different best friend. The sweetest friend of all.

The LORD is close to the brokenhearted and saves those who are crushed in spirit.

PSALM 34:18

WEEK 40.
ON GOD'S STRENGTH ALONE

SCRIPTURE READING:
DANIEL 3

What is impossible with men is possible with God.

LUKE 18:27

Krista Barrows loved to shop. Even more, she loved that these days she could drive to the mall by herself. Just after her seventeenth birthday, she'd bought a used Toyota, and now, with her parents' permission, she was free to shop whenever the need arose.

She'd been looking for an engraved picture frame for her boyfriend when she heard the announcement that the mall was closing. Krista headed for the cash register and wondered how it could have gotten so late. She recalled her mother's warning: "If you'll be late, take a friend. Mall parking lots are dangerous after hours."

Hurry, Krista, she told herself. Why hadn't she brought her mother's cell phone? That way she could at least call and tell her parents she was on her way.

Once outside the mall, Krista walked across the dark, cold parking lot, fumbling for her keys between three bags. Lost in her search, she barely noticed in her peripheral vision something move up ahead near her car. Finally her fingers wrapped around her keys. When she looked up, the parking lot was empty. She glanced about, her heart beating faster. Then she picked up her pace, took quick steps toward her Toyota, opened the door, and climbed inside.

Suddenly, a masked man appeared a few feet from her window. His eyes were wild and he was pointing a gun at her. He took a few hurried steps toward her car and motioned for her to open the door. With trembling hands, Krista locked her door and tried to start the car. Nothing happened. The man banged his gun against her window as Krista turned the key again. Again, silence. The engine was dead.

"Please, God!" she whispered. "I need your help!"

The man smashed his gun against her window another time, this time cracking the glass. Closing her eyes, Krista tried once more to start the car, and finally the engine turned over. In an instant, Krista slammed the car into gear and sped off, leaving the man in the shadows.

Krista cried the entire way home. What had the man wanted from her? How long had he been waiting by her car? Even stranger, why hadn't her car started the first time? The engine was in perfect condition according to their family's mechanic. *Whatever happened back there, God, thanks for getting me through it.*

She was still shaking when she pulled into her driveway, shut off the engine, and headed up the walkway. A shudder worked its way through her as she imagined the things that man might have done if he'd been able to break her window and get inside. Still feeling weak, she made her way inside the house. There she tearfully shared the incident with her parents.

Immediately, her father called the police. When he'd made the report, he turned to Krista. "You're safe now," he told her as he hugged her tight.

"But I thought . . ." Krista's crying became sobs.

"God was looking out for you, honey." Her mother reached out and took her hand. "He helped you get away. . . . I have no doubt about that."

Krista's father cocked his head. "You say the car wouldn't start?"

"Right. It was weird, Dad. Like it was

251

broken."

"Let's go take a look at it." Her father grabbed a flashlight and led the way back outside to Krista's parked car. "I can't understand why it would have done that. The mechanic just checked it a few weeks ago."

"I know. I thought it was strange, too." Krista stood beside him, her knees still shaking.

Her father opened the hood and aimed the flashlight inside. For a long while he stood there, saying nothing. Then he took a step back as the flashlight fell slowly to his side. His eyes were wide, his mouth open.

"What's wrong?" Krista looked from her father to the car and back again.

"It's impossible," he muttered.

"What?" Krista moved closer, looking under the car's hood.

"There." Her father pointed the flashlight once more at the engine. "The battery is gone."

"What?" Krista was confused. "Can a car run without a battery?"

A strange chuckle came from her father. "That's just it. It's impossible."

"So how did I . . ."

Her father shook his head and lifted his eyes to hers. "Don't you see? Someone set you up. While you were shopping, they took your battery and waited for you. They knew you wouldn't be able to start your car and . . ." Her father stopped mid-sentence, and Krista guessed he was imagining what the masked man had intended. "It's impossible," he said again.

"I don't understand," Krista said, more confused than ever. "If the battery is gone, how did the car start?"

"That's what I mean. There isn't any way to start this engine without a battery."

Chills coursed down Krista's spine and she reached for her father's hand. "What are you saying?"

"I don't know. I can't explain it. Somehow you made it home without a battery. It's impossible."

Suddenly Krista felt a peace wash over her. "Could it be that God was watching out for me?"

Her father's eyes widened and a knowing look came over his face. Slowly, deliberately, he stared up at the star-covered sky. Krista followed his example, and for several minutes they gazed into the night. Finally, her father broke the silence. "God, we may never understand what happened tonight," he whispered. "But we are eternally grateful. Thank you."

By faith we understand that the universe was formed at God's command, so that what is seen was not made out of what was visible.

HEBREWS 11:3

WEEK 41.
A PRAYER EACH DAY

SCRIPTURE READING:
PROVERBS 2

We know that in all things God works for the good of those who love him, who have been called according to his purpose.

ROMANS 8:28

Cindy Henning was only sixteen when she got the shattering news: she was pregnant. She'd been warned against dating the college boy, but things had gotten out of hand. When she called him, he said, "Get an abortion. Otherwise, don't call me again."

Cindy never did.

When she was four months pregnant, she determined to keep the baby. The life inside her was her very own child. Finally, unable to hide the truth any longer, she told her parents. But despite Cindy's tears and protests, there was no way they would allow her to raise the baby.

After a few days, Cindy realized she was too young to move out on her own or care for a baby. Without her parents' support, she could do nothing but follow their orders. When she realized she would hand her child to another woman, the tears flowed.

"Please, God, whatever happens to my baby, help us find our way back together."

Her parents sent her to live with friends three states away. The months passed quickly. At her seven-month appointment she found out the baby was a girl. She called her "Baby Girl" and often prayed over her.

Every moment of her daughter's birth happened in a strange sort of slow motion, the images sharp, pressing into her mind in a way she would remember forever — March 13, 1983. After the baby's first cries, for the sweetest minutes she'd ever known, she cradled her child to her chest, looking at her, seeing past her eyes to the toddler and little girl and teenager her baby would one day become. She drank in the full sensation.

The infant's eyes were open, and they seemed to be asking her the question that would long haunt her. *Why? Why would you give me away?*

"Cindy?" The social worker stepped into the room. "It's time."

The adoption was closed, so Cindy wouldn't meet her baby's new parents. She drew in the faint sweet smell of her daughter, the warm weight of her against her chest. Then she kissed her daughter's cheek and whispered, "I love you, Baby Girl." Then she looked at the woman and out came the greatest lie she'd ever spoken: "I'm ready."

The ache was immediate and constant. Long after Cindy returned home, she missed her daughter with an intensity that frightened her.

Five years later she fell in love with a man who was everything her first boyfriend hadn't been — honest, faithful, and driven to make a life for himself through both integrity and character. Two years later they married. From the beginning she told him about the baby girl and how badly she wanted to meet her someday.

"I'll pray about it," her husband said. "One day you'll find her if that's God's plan."

The years went by and Cindy and her husband had three daughters — each one a bittersweet reminder of all Cindy had lost with her first child. More time passed and Cindy never stopped believing that somehow, someway, God would answer her prayer even though the adoption paperwork remained closed.

One afternoon after a morning in which her firstborn girl was heavy on her heart, Cindy headed to a parent-teacher conference with Mrs. Barnett, her youngest daughter's fifth-grade teacher. Mrs. Barnett had just explained that a new student teacher would be with them the rest of the year when the classroom door opened and a beautiful young woman walked in. Cindy looked at her, and everything seemed to freeze.

Cindy stood slowly, her eyes locked on the young woman. Everything about her was as familiar as the faces around her dinner table each night. Cindy said the only thing she could think to say: "Were you adopted?"

The subtle confusion in the woman's eyes cleared instantly. Her mouth hung open for a few seconds and slowly, she nodded. "Yes. I was born March 13, 1983."

A cry came from Cindy's mouth. "I think . . . I think you're my daughter."

The young woman didn't speak. Certainty shone in her expression and rather than compare notes, she came to Cindy and the two fell into each other's arms. It was an embrace that erased the years in a single moment, one that convinced Cindy she was on holy ground because this was a miracle like no other.

"Baby Girl," Cindy whispered. "I prayed for you every day."

"I'm Anna." Tears glistened in her eyes. "And I've had the most wonderful life. I've prayed for this, too. So that I could thank you in person for what you did."

The conference forgotten, Cindy and Anna caught up on the twenty-two years they'd been apart. Anna explained that she had been raised by a loving family who had prayed that Anna would meet her birth mother one day.

Anna took Cindy's hand. "I always believed that somehow we'd meet. Because I was afraid you might've regretted giving me up." She looked deeper into Cindy's eyes. "And I never wanted that. Not when God allowed me the greatest life with my adopted parents."

Cindy held her daughter again and allowed herself to cry, not for the years she'd lost, but for the perfect way God had worked everything out.

"Can I ask you something?" Anna stepped back.

"Yes. Ask anything."

"I'd like to meet my other sisters."

With that another certainty grew in Cindy's heart. She would never again wonder about her daughter or where she was or how her life was going. Because forever more she would be a part of her life.

And that was the greatest miracle of all.

Look at the nations and watch — and be utterly amazed. For I am going to do something in your days that you would not believe, even if you were told.

HABAKKUK 1:5

Week 42.
The Face of Jesus
SCRIPTURE READING:
ACTS 19:1–22

I am convinced that neither death nor life,
neither angels nor demons, . . . nor any
powers, . . . nor anything else in all cre-
ation, will be able to separate us from the
love of God that is in Christ Jesus our Lord.
ROMANS 8:38–39

Steve Getz had dabbled with drugs since
eighth grade, but the summer he turned
sixteen he was using heavily. An hour before
coming to the market, he had taken a
mixture of illegal drugs, and suddenly the
walls of the market seemed to be melting
and the fruit and vegetables had turned into
large bloblike substances that were coming
toward him.

"Help!" he screamed. Then he began running full speed through the store, up one
aisle and down another, until the store
manager and a customer forced him to the
ground. Steve struggled to break free. The
hallucinations were worse than ever.

Steve closed his eyes but when he opened them, he screamed in terror. Horrible, dark demons were coming toward him. They had fierce expressions and fangs that dripped with blood. There were small demons floating near his face and laughing at him, and there were monstrous demons circling him. It was utter evil, a death and destruction he was powerless to escape.

The customer, who had been holding Steve's arms, leaned in closer to him. "You're going to be okay."

"Help me!" Steve shouted.

"Open your eyes, Steve." The man's voice was soothing and clear. With all the concentration he could muster, Steve forced himself to listen above the noise of the gathering crowd. "Steve, you can trust me."

Steve opened his eyes slowly. As the picture cleared, the demons were still there but were retreating. And in the center of the picture was what appeared to be the face of Jesus Christ. It was the same face he'd seen in his Bible storybook from church. Awestruck, Steven stopped twisting and struggling and grew calm. As he stared, the Christlike face began to speak: "Do you want to be free from the demons, Steve?"

Suddenly, Steve began to cry. "Yes," he spoke softly. He had to get free from the drugs . . . before it was too late. "Please help me."

The man in the picture smiled. "No more drugs, Steve. With them come the demons. It is your choice."

"No, I can't do it by myself!" Steve screamed and started to struggle again. But the man seemed to possess an inhuman strength. "Help me. Please."

The demons were completely gone. Only the image of a pure and radiant Christ filled the center of his vision. "Steve, you won't have to do this by yourself. If you want to be free, turn to me. I will always be right there to help you. Just call me and I will be with you."

"Lord." Steve whispered the word, not sure if he was still hallucinating, but savoring the peace he felt. *Is that you, God? Are you really here, talking with me?*

Slowly the image began to fade. But before it disappeared altogether, he heard the voice once more. "Yes, Steve, it is I. I will be here for you."

Suddenly Steve felt extremely tired. He closed his eyes and his body went limp.

The customer who had been talking quietly to Steve turned to the store manager and said, "I think you can handle it now. The worst is over."

"Thanks," the manager said, shaking the customer's hand. Then he reached over and pinned Steve's arms down. When he looked around, the customer had vanished and the paramedics and police were arriving.

Before the police took him away, Steve found out the customer was already gone. "Please, tell me what he looked like, the man who talked to me."

The manager said, "He had short blond hair, a muscular build, and . . . a real clean-shaven face. That's all I can remember."

Steve shook his head. "No, I mean the man who helped me. He had dark hair, a beard, and brown eyes."

The manager shook his head. "Maybe it was the drugs, son. The guy who helped you was blond."

After Steve was booked and released by the police, his mother took him home. Steve had been in and out of a rehabilitation center twice since his thirteenth birthday, and now this. His mother and father prayed for him every day, but it had been years since he'd talked about God. Where would he ever get the strength to leave the drugs behind?

Normally after he'd gotten into trouble because of drug use, Steve was defiant and angry. But as he described to his mother what had happened in detail, tears filled his eyes. When he told her the words he'd heard the man speak, she whispered, "Steve, that's amazing."

"I know that guy was sent by God to warn me. If I don't accept God's help now and change my life, the demons will get me."

"Son," his mother said, "it's a miracle. You were given a message from God the same way people used to get them back in biblical times — from angels. Maybe the man who talked to you was an angel, telling you what the Lord wanted you to hear."

Steve thought a moment. "I'll never touch drugs again, Mom. I'm going to turn to God and give him my life. It's going to change my life. I promise you that."

Steve checked with the manager several times regarding the man who helped him. But though the man was never seen again, his work was not in vain.

Steve kept his word. For the next twenty years and to this day, Steve Getz has stayed away from all drugs. He has also maintained a dynamic relationship with God, one that began on a cold supermarket floor in the grasp of a man who was, perhaps, an angel.

When they came to Jesus, they saw the man who had been possessed by the legion of demons, sitting there, dressed and in his right mind; and they were afraid.

MARK 5:15

WEEK 43.
BACK TOGETHER AGAIN

SCRIPTURE READING:
ACTS 23:12–35

Rescue me, O LORD, from evil men; protect me from men of violence.

PSALM 140:1

Scott Miller was forever second-guessing himself as a single father. His wife had left him and their daughter and son fifteen years ago, and now both were teenagers.

It was Friday night, which for years had been family night. But when Laura turned sixteen, her friends had something fun going on every night. Scott had laid down the law.

"You're too young to be out more than once a week."

Most of the time Laura agreed. But that night her two favorite girlfriends asked her to go shopping, even though a party was planned for the next night.

"Please, Dad? It's just for a few hours."

"You know the rule, Laura. Once a week."

"Yeah, but this isn't a night thing, it's

shopping."

He could feel his determination beginning to crumble. Times like this he wondered why he'd never remarried — someone who could be a mother for Laura. For a moment he wondered about Becky Olsen, his first love. She wouldn't have walked out on them. She'd be here. "Who's driving?"

"Susie's mother will pick me up and drop me off."

"Okay," he said. She'd be fine; this was Mill Creek, Washington, with one of the nation's lowest crime rates.

"Thanks, Daddy. I promise I won't be long."

Becky Olsen was a sales manager for the largest pharmaceutical company in the nation. Although her territory was southern Oregon and California, she'd agreed to take meetings in Seattle on the weekend.

She was single, and work hid her loneliness. Six years earlier, her husband and sons had been killed in a car-train accident. It took two years for Becky to get back to work, and she did it with a determination to remain single. She'd loved once, and lost. That was enough. The problem was the dreaded loneliness. Not for another family. She wanted a friend.

Becky found herself occasionally wondering how her high school boyfriend, Scott Miller, was doing. They'd been young, but he had been one of her best friends.

Her thoughts cleared and she thought about the business at hand. She needed to pick up a pair of nylons. It was almost eight o'clock when she pulled into a mall parking lot just north of Seattle.

Becky's attention was immediately taken by a man in dark clothing walking behind a teenage girl. The girl's eyes were terror-stricken. And why was he walking so close behind her? Was he pushing her? They reached a beat-up sedan that looked out of place at the high-end mall.

God, what's going on? Is the girl in trouble? Follow them, daughter. Follow.

The answer was not an audible voice, but it resonated in Becky's heart as if God had shouted the words with a bullhorn. When the car pulled away, she stayed reasonably close behind. Becky's heart raced as they turned onto the main road. The girl must be in trouble. But if she called for help, the police would want a reason. When the man turned onto a less-traveled street, she knew if he led them into a deserted area, he'd see her following him. Without another thought, she dialed 911.

"Nine-one-one. What's your emergency?"

"I'm following a man who I believe has kidnapped a teenage girl. She looked scared to death."

Three minutes later, a police car passed Becky and pulled over the sedan. Becky stopped and watched the drama play out. While patting the man down, the officer pulled a gun from the man's pocket. Within seconds the man was cuffed and placed in the back of the squad car.

Becky climbed out of her car, her knees trembling. She approached the car, where officers were talking to the girl, and explained that she had called in the incident.

The teenager was sobbing, shaking from fear. "I forgot my wallet in the car. So I went out to get it and I felt something against my waist." She sobbed twice. "It was his gun. He told me to start walking or he'd shoot."

Becky felt the color drain from her face.

The girl got out of the car and shook Becky's hand. "Thank you so much." She folded her arms and began to shiver. "My dad is on the way. Could you wait? He'll want to thank you, too."

Becky agreed. Five minutes passed and finally a Jeep pulled up. It was dark, but Becky watched as a tall man ran toward them. His eyes were locked on the girl.

"Laura . . . thank God!" He took her in his arms.

Becky stepped back, intent on saying good-bye and getting on her way. But the girl pulled from her father's arms. "You have to meet Becky. She called for help."

The man turned to Becky, and suddenly they both froze. Becky stared at his face and gasped quietly.

"Becky? How did you —"

"I'm here on business. I can't believe this."

Laura was watching. "You know each other?"

"Yes. In fact, we do." Scott gave Becky a hug.

In a matter of minutes, Scott and Becky learned that each was single, and that they'd been wondering about each other for years. They drove to a diner to catch up.

"We were part of a miracle tonight," Laura said as she sipped her drink. "God brought you two friends together, and he did it by having Becky save my life. Only God does that sort of stuff."

Scott and Becky agreed Laura was right. And they still remind themselves often of that miracle, especially each June when they celebrate their wedding anniversary.

After two days he will revive us; on the

third day he will restore us, that we may live in his presence.

HOSEA 6:2

WEEK 44.
A CHILD FROM HEAVEN

SCRIPTURE READING: GENESIS 15

Little children were brought to Jesus for him to place his hands on them and pray for them.

MATTHEW 19:13

With their entire hearts Ben and Beverly Jameson wanted to be parents, but nothing they had tried through medical means had done anything to help Beverly get pregnant. They contacted a private adoption attorney and learned that the cost would be approximately twelve thousand dollars — money they simply didn't have. Finally they contacted their bank and took out a second mortgage on their house.

Ben was a manager at a local supermarket. Beverly worked as a teacher's assistant, but once they adopted she planned to quit and spend her days at home. If things got tight financially, Ben would take a second job.

The process took six months, and one afternoon they took the call they'd been waiting for. A homeless couple had contacted the Jamesons' attorney and informed him that they wanted to give their baby up for adoption. The family was quickly matched with Ben and Beverly, and three weeks later their son, Eric, came home. Their attorney also told them that the homeless woman had gotten her tubes tied after delivering Eric. He would never have a biological sibling.

Beverly quit her job and became a full-time mother. Eric was the child of their dreams — a dark-haired, half-Hispanic child who loved them from the beginning.

The trouble didn't start until Eric was three years old. Multiple bruises on Eric's back and shoulders were followed by a high temperature, then a trip to the doctor and blood tests.

Within a week they found out Eric had leukemia. His blood type wasn't listed in the bone marrow donor banks, so his family could pray for just one thing — that somehow someone would enter the registry as a match to Eric — a possibility that carried with it odds of twenty thousand to one.

The wait was terrible.

The Jamesons had none of the money needed to hold local blood drives, events that could add hundreds or thousands of names to the national registry. They met with their pastor one Sunday and explained how dire the situation had become.

Tears filled Ben's eyes. "Even if we find a match, I'm not sure we could pay for it."

The pastor organized an event with a sister church, and in one weekend they raised enough money for the Jamesons to pay their part of the bone marrow transplant cost. But they hadn't found anyone to match little Eric's blood and bone marrow type.

Siblings had a 50 percent chance of being a match, so that was an option Beverly wanted to hold on to. But the woman hadn't had children before Eric; and after having her tubes tied, she certainly wouldn't have more.

Another month passed and Eric seemed to grow stronger. His doctor confirmed that he was in remission but warned that the remission was only temporary. Often when a child with leukemia slips out of remission, his disease is more aggressive, worse than before.

Ben and Beverly kept praying.

Then one day a few weeks later, they took a call that stopped their world. Despite the fact that she'd had her tubes tied, Eric's birth mother had given birth to a little girl a year after Eric was born.

"At first the woman wanted to keep the little girl. But her husband has a drug problem. They've been on the streets ever since the child was born. She's two now. The woman is pretty sure she wants to give the girl up, and there's only one place she would want her to be — with you and Ben. She'll let us know next week."

Beverly and Ben prayed desperately on multiple fronts. First, that if it was God's will, the woman would agree to give up her daughter. Second, if they could bring this little girl home, that her blood would be a perfect match for Eric.

"It seems like too much to ask," Beverly said.

"But we have a God who loves doing the impossible," Ben reminded her.

Over the next few days, they survived on faith alone. Eric stayed in remission, but he was pale, thinner than he should have been. With every passing hour it was obvious he would need a bone marrow transplant one day soon.

But while they waited, their pastor and the sister church that helped raise money for the Jamesons all prayed around the clock. Finally the news came — the woman had decided to give up her little girl. Ben and Beverly rejoiced in the addition of a daughter to their family. They were shocked to see how much Eric and his sister looked alike.

The little girl's name was Corinne, and the Jamesons chose to keep her name the same. That way she would have one less adjustment to make. Once she'd been home for a week, the doctor drew the blood to test her prospects as a donor for Eric.

By then, Beverly was convinced that a miracle was at hand. The sister who never should have been had wound up in their home. If they looked that much alike, of course their bone marrow would match. And sure enough, when they received word from their doctor they weren't surprised.

Eric's miracle little sister was indeed a match!

The operation was not a risk for a toddler, so the procedure was arranged and a month later the bone marrow transplant took place. Today, fifteen years later, Eric and Corinne are the best of friends. The miracle of Corinne's life lives on in her brother, and Ben and Beverly are grateful every day for the answered prayers that came their way, the brilliant morning that followed the darkest night of all.

Everything is possible for him who believes.

MARK 9:23

Week 45.
The Miracle of Life

SCRIPTURE READING:
PSALM 139:1–16

When God created man, he made him in the likeness of God.

GENESIS 5:1

Kendra Cottner spent a decade battling to protect the rights of the unborn, and eventually her convictions led her to a position as president of the National Women's Coalition for Life. She was often asked a hypothetical question: "If your baby was severely handicapped, wouldn't you want the choice to abort?"

And always Kendra would shake her head. "Life comes from God. He has a reason for each of us."

Then she married Peter, a podiatrist, and they spent three years battling infertility and praying for a child. When they learned Kendra was pregnant, they rejoiced. Then four months into the pregnancy, she discovered she was carrying twins, one boy, one girl. But the girl didn't seem to be developing properly, so more tests were done. Over the next four weeks, Kendra learned that the female twin had a severe birth defect in which most of the brain develops outside the skull in a sac at the base of the neck.

"I'm so sorry," the doctor said. "There's nothing we can do because the baby has no protection for her brain stem. This condition is fatal because any distress to the brain stem causes immediate death in most cases."

Kendra allowed the tears to come. *Help us, God,* she prayed silently. *Work a miracle.*

"I'd suggest we perform a selective abortion," the doctor continued. "That way there would be plenty of fluid and room for the other twin to develop."

"You want us to abort her?" Kendra said, astonished.

"Mrs. Adams, she isn't going to live. Why go through the trauma of carrying two babies only to have one of them die at birth?"

Kendra shook her head in disbelief. "Doctor, I can feel her kicking. She may not have a long life but she will have a safe and comfortable one. Abortion is out of the question."

The couple left the office in tears, and almost immediately Kendra began trying to resolve the dilemma.

"Let's name her Anne Marie," Kendra suggested on the ride home. "Saint Marie was also a very sickly child, but God had a plan for her life anyway."

Peter nodded. "Let's get everyone we know to pray."

In the next few weeks Kendra and Peter made phone calls to dozens of people, who in turn called others, so that in time hundreds of people from churches across the country were praying for Anne Marie.

Next, Kendra researched Anne's condition online and learned about doctors and support groups that specialized in neural defects. She spoke with neonatologists and neurosurgeons to learn all she could.

In the sixth month of her pregnancy, Kendra quit working so her body could rest. Specialists said that additional rest might make the difference in whether Anne Marie survived the pregnancy. Now, as she prayed for a miracle for Anne Marie, she felt no less certain that the baby was worthy of life. But gradually, as the weeks wore on, tests showed that the defect was so serious that doctors doubted the baby would survive the pregnancy.

But week after week Anne Marie survived. By the end of the second trimester, Kendra and Peter had a highly trained neonatal team scheduled to deliver the twins by cesarean section, since labor would be fatal to little Anne.

When Kendra was nearly eight months pregnant, she was sitting in church when she was overcome with the thought that she was praying with the wrong intentions. Suddenly she heard what seemed to be a voice of authority telling her to pray for peace, not miracles.

"All right, Lord," she prayed quietly. "I pray for peace and acceptance. If there is a reason why this has to be, then I will trust you."

In the next six weeks she focused her energy in a different direction. If Anne died at birth, then she and Peter would need help dealing with the loss. She contacted organizations that dealt with the loss of a child in multiple births, and others that helped parents handle the death of a young child.

There was one more thing. She talked with Peter one night, and the next morning she called the Regional Organ Bank of Michigan. She explained Anne's situation at length and recalled the recent death of their friends' son who had been on a waiting list for a heart valve transplant.

"We want our little girl to make the difference in another child's life," she said finally.

Now she was certain Anne Marie's life would have a purpose.

Finally, the morning for the scheduled cesarean section arrived. At 9:20 a.m. Jeffrey was delivered and let out a healthy cry. A minute later, Anne Marie was placed protectively in Peter's arms as doctors worked to stitch up Kendra's abdomen.

"It's worse than I thought," the neonatologist said as he examined Anne. "She's dying."

Peter nodded and smiled tearfully at both his parents and Kendra's parents, who had come to hold Anne before she died.

Anne Marie was passed from one grandparent to the next so each could whisper to the baby, telling her how much they loved her and that they would see her one day in heaven.

The medication and recovery from surgery made it impossible for Kendra to hold her right away, so Peter cradled Anne in his arms when the grandparents had had their turns.

"Anne, we will always love you," Peter whispered into the deep blue eyes of his little girl. "You will always be a part of this family and someday we'll all be together again."

Finally, six hours after she was born, Anne

gazed once more into her father's eyes and drew her last breath. Shortly afterward, Kendra's medication wore off and she awoke. Only then did she get to hold Anne.

"Watch over us from heaven, little one," Kendra cried softly. "We will never forget you."

Two days later, Kendra and Peter were notified by the organ bank that Anne's heart valves had been used to save the lives of two critically ill children in Chicago.

Weeks passed before Kendra could talk about Anne with anyone. Only then, after hours of prayer for peace and acceptance, did she come to terms with Anne's short life. Today she devotes some of her time to helping other parents find peace in the tragedy of losing a child. She reminds people: "The best we can hope for with any of our children is not the kind of career they choose or where they will live or how much money they will make. The best we can hope for is that our children make it to heaven and touch the lives of others along the way. As for us, Anne is already safely home. Not only that, but in passing through this world she gave life to two terminally ill children.

"How many of us can say that, even after living a hundred years?"

Before I was born the LORD called me;
from my birth he has made mention of my
name.

ISAIAH 49:1

WEEK 46.
HEAVENLY
PROTECTION

SCRIPTURE READING:
PSALM 5

When you walk through the fire, you will not be burned; the flames will not set you ablaze.

ISAIAH 43:2

Barbara Evans had eyed the house in the Santa Monica mountains for ten years. It was a Victorian with a stunning view of the Pacific Ocean and it left her breathless.

"That's my dream house," she told her husband, Ted. "If it's ever for sale, I'd love to own it."

At the time it was only a dream, but as Ted did increasingly better with his business, the idea of affording such a house became a reality.

On an anniversary, Ted told Barbara, "I'd give you the moon if I could."

Barbara laughed. "I'd settle for the house on the hill."

Ten years went by and Barbara gave up on the idea that it would ever be for sale.

Then, one month when she was in Vermont, the dream house went on the market. Ted worked frantically with a realtor and two weeks later when Barbara returned, Ted handed her a key at the airport.

"I have a surprise for you," he told her. "Because I never want you to doubt how much I love you."

Six weeks later they were settled in. "It's everything I dreamed it would be," she whispered to Ted. "But it wouldn't be anything without you."

Five years passed and one hot August Sunday a firestorm raged through the Santa Monica mountains. Barbara was visiting her sister in the San Fernando Valley. When Ted returned from church, he could see smoke. And he prayed that God would keep their home from danger.

About two hours later, he smelled smoke and looked out his window. The fire had gained ground and seemed to be heading in his direction. Ted went outside to watch the fire's progress and was joined by his neighbor Roy. Despite the dry brush that surrounded their homes, they felt certain that firefighters would contain the blaze.

Ted decided to gather old pictures and other irreplaceable items and packed them into his car, and Roy went to water his roof down.

Then Ted called Barbara. "Honey, the fire's close. Pray."

Barbara hung up the phone and bowed her head. "God, please keep my love letter from Ted safe." Then she had an image of a circle of protection. "Lord, place a hedge of protection around Ted and our home. Circle it with your angels."

Meanwhile, Ted began spraying water on his deck with his garden hose. Since he had no ladder that would reach his roof, he could not saturate it as he would've liked to.

Then suddenly the wind changed directions and sent the fire directly toward Ted's house. Almost immediately, Roy came racing back to Ted's house. Together the men stood, trancelike, as they stared in horror at the approaching wall of flames some thirty feet high, consuming everything in its path and gaining strength.

"We're in big trouble," Ted muttered as the ferocious blaze leaped over a gorge and moved up the hillside toward their homes.

"Come on!" Roy screamed. "Run for your life!"

Ted dropped his hose and the two men began running. The men jumped into their cars and sped away. Once he got to a parking lot on the beach below, Ted stopped his car and stepped out. Other fleeing homeowners did the same. All they could see was a fog of flames and smoke where the structures should have been.

Ted felt helpless and sorrowful, but at that instant a Bible verse came to mind: *"In all things, God works for the good of those who love him."* Ted closed his eyes and forced himself to believe that promise. With everything disintegrating in flames, he was determined that his faith would stand.

As the fire moved closer, firefighters told the group to head for shelter farther down the highway. Ted walked back to his car as a young man approached him.

"Hey!" he called, speaking to Ted. "Don't worry. I got on your roof and watered it down for you."

With flames crashing into the Evanses' yard, that wasn't possible. Convinced that the man must have confused him with someone else, Ted said, "Well, thanks. I sure appreciate that."

The man nodded and walked away as Ted climbed into his car and drove to the place where evacuees were being directed. Then he called Barbara and told her the bad news.

"Thank God you're all right," was all she

said. "I care more about you than the house."

The fire continued to burn through the night, and no one had word on the status of the houses. Then, late that night, he remembered some friends who lived across the valley and could see the Evanses' house. He called them immediately.

"You won't believe it, Ted. We saw the flames change direction and head right for your house. Our family formed a prayer circle and prayed for your safety and the safety of your house." The man paused. "Your house looks absolutely untouched."

Ted thanked his friend but was convinced the man had mistaken his house for another. It was impossible.

The next morning, it was safe to return. When he arrived home Ted was stunned by what he saw: his friend had been right.

The ferocious fire had burned to within ten feet of his house and then abruptly stopped. All around his house the brush and wood were destroyed, but the house was untouched. The power lines that fed electricity into the house were melted and telephone lines were fused together. Even their expansive wooden deck was only lightly scorched.

Then Ted spotted the hose he had dropped

on his deck — it was now draped up over the house and lying on the roof.

When Barbara got home later that day, they clung to each other and wept.

In all, there were seven houses along the narrow, hilly road where Barbara and Ted lived. Three were completely destroyed and three seriously damaged. Only the Evanses' house stood undamaged in any way, in the middle of a house-sized piece of the hillside that alone remained unburned.

In the weeks that followed, Barbara spent a great deal of time wondering why their house had been spared. Research told her that the heat would have had to have been 1,800 degrees or hotter in order to melt the power lines. With temperatures that hot, the house should have burst into flames by spontaneous combustion from the heat alone. Yet not only was it unburned, but it was also undamaged in any way.

They later learned that three witnesses had seen someone on the Evanses' roof watering it down after Ted and Roy fled the area. Yet there was no ladder with which to climb on the roof, and no way water could have flowed from the Evanses' well since power lines had been melted, thereby cutting off electricity to the water pump.

"I prayed God would send a hedge of

protection." Barbara smiled through her tears. "He sent an angel of mercy to save the greatest gift Ted had ever given me."

In all their distress he too was distressed, and the angel of his presence saved them. In his love and mercy he redeemed them; he lifted them up and carried them all the days of old.

ISAIAH 63:9

WEEK 47.
THANKS FOR A MOTHER'S LOVE

SCRIPTURE READING:
JUDGES 6:33–40

If now I have found favor in your eyes, give me a sign that it is really you talking to me.

JUDGES 6:17

After decades of a strained and tense relationship, Molly Benson and her daughter Peg had enjoyed ten years of closeness. There were afternoon walks and long conversations where they bared their hearts and dreams. But when Molly entered her early sixties, she was diagnosed with degenerative muscle and connective-tissue disorders that cause a gradual wasting of the body and eventually result in death.

When Molly learned of the diagnosis, she shared the news with her three grown children. "Pray that I don't leave any of you until God himself is ready to take me."

As the year passed, Molly's condition worsened. She lost use of her arms and legs and was eventually confined to a wheelchair.

During that time, Peg's brother and sister moved away to start their own families. Peg and her husband, Rick, stayed behind to care for Molly.

"I don't know what I'd do without you, Peg," her mother told her on several occasions. "You are more than I ever could have hoped for in a daughter."

Molly spent much of her time with Peg and Rick. Every day was filled with joy, because of the close relationship she had not only with Peg but also with Peg's children, Molly's precious grandchildren. Although she couldn't do the more physical things she'd hoped to do as a grandmother, she could tell them stories and listen to them when they played make-believe.

When Molly hit her sixty-second birthday, she was completely crippled and the disease had settled in her lungs, making it hard to breathe. The doctors had warned that she might not live through the year. During those days, Peg would watch her mother sleeping and wonder how she was going to deal with the woman's inevitable death.

Then, almost overnight, her condition worsened dramatically and she had to be hospitalized for lung congestion. Peg kept a vigil at her mother's bedside, praying for her and singing familiar, comforting songs.

Although Molly's entire body was affected by her diseases, her mind was perfectly intact. Soon she could barely talk, but many times she would look at Peg in such a way that Peg was sure her mother was listening.

On the day before Thanksgiving, her mother seemed worse than ever. Peg held her mother's hand tightly in her own. "I want you to know how much we all love you, Mom. And I want you to know that we'll all be together again someday."

Looking up toward heaven, Peg began to pray. "Dear God our Father, thank you for my mother's love. Help us find a way to survive without her."

Her mother remained still, but her eyes filled with tears. Then, very peacefully, she slipped into a coma. Finally, at 12:15 a.m. on Thanksgiving Day, she died.

At the exact moment, Peg knew that the body before her no longer housed her mother's spirit. A tremendous peace, like something she'd never known before, came over her. Life would be hard without her mother, but Peg had the assurance that things had worked out for the best. Everything was going to be okay.

Peg agreed with her siblings to take care of all the remaining business involving their mother's death. After the funeral, the whirlwind of activity quieted down and in the weeks that followed the peace that had helped her through the initial days all but disappeared. Instead, Peg felt desperately lonely and overwhelmed with the idea of selling her mother's house and the work left to do.

One night, as she felt she was drowning in grief, she began to pray, "Sweet Lord, please help me to feel your peace again. I believe Mom is with you now, but help me to really know it in my heart. Let me know everything's going to be okay."

Early the next day the phone rang. Just before Peg picked up the cordless phone, she realized that the other phone in the next room was not ringing.

"Hello?" When there was only silence, she hung up.

An hour later, the phone rang again, but only the cordless phone. Peg answered but no one was there.

Nearly two hours later, once again only the cordless phone rang but no one was there. This time Peg unplugged the phone from the electrical outlet, knowing it couldn't ring without electricity feeding the phone's base unit.

Thirty minutes later, the cordless phone rang again. It seemed impossible. No one answered.

Peg hung up and pulled the phone away from the wall and bundled up the detached cording. Mentally she made a note to take the unit in for repair.

Another hour passed as Peg sifted through paperwork regarding her mother's death. "This is hard, Lord," she said with a sigh, feeling tears once again gathering in her eyes. "I miss her so badly."

Suddenly the early afternoon silence was broken by the ringing of the telephone — not the wall phone. She followed the sound and felt a chill run through her body.

The cordless phone — no longer attached to either the electrical outlet or the phone jack — was ringing. Peg gingerly picked up the receiver.

"Hello?" Peg's voice was soft, uncertain. Once again there was only silence at the other end.

Suddenly Peg remembered the date. It was December 11, her mother's birthday.

Instantly she was flooded by the same feeling of peace that had washed over her the moment her mother had died. She thought about the prayer she had said the night before and knew that God had answered her. Everything really was going to be okay.

May the God of hope fill you with all joy and peace as you trust in him, so that you may overflow with hope by the power of the Holy Spirit.

ROMANS 15:13

WEEK 48.
ONE MORE DAY

SCRIPTURE READING:
ISAIAH 38

For you who revere my name, the sun of righteousness will rise with healing in its wings.

MALACHI 4:2

At age sixteen, Julie Keller wanted nothing more than for her twin brother, Jared, to live another year . . . one more Christmas, one more spring, one more summer. But that August night she found herself in a hospital room begging God for one more day.

Jared had been born with cystic fibrosis, a debilitating lung disease — an illness that would take his life eventually. The doctors had told the family he'd be lucky to live to his mid-twenties.

Julie's parents did not believe in God, or in prayer, or in miracles. But when Julie and Jared were thirteen, they went to a Young Life camp, had given their lives to God, and found rides to church every week. When

Jared was sick and couldn't attend church or school, he'd tell Julie, "Keep praying for me. Save a spot at the lunch table, okay?" They had this conversation many times.

A person with cystic fibrosis lives with the constant threat of pneumonia, and over the years Jared had suffered with pneumonia many times. After attending another Young Life camp, he came down with the worst case ever and was rushed to the hospital.

That had been two days ago. Now, doctors had just met with the Kellers and told them it didn't look as though Jared would make it this time. Julie's parents held on to each other and wept, and while she wanted to ask them to pray for a miracle, she knew from the past that they would shut her down.

When her parents went to the cafeteria for some coffee, Julie stayed to pray. *God, don't let my brother die. The two of us share everything,* she prayed silently. That had been true since they were small children, but especially since they entered high school. Because Julie was popular and outgoing, Jared was constantly showered with attention and friendships as well.

"It's so cool," one of Julie's friends had said the week before at youth camp, "how you and your brother are best friends. I wish

I had something like that with my brother."

Now, after the greatest week together in their lives at camp, it looked as if she might lose Jared. The thought tore at Julie's heart and made it hard for her to breathe. She wanted to leave the waiting room and go to Jared's room, but the doctor had asked them to let him rest.

"Lord," Julie whispered, "please help my brother. I love him so much, and I know he's scared. Please help him breathe. Make the pneumonia go away."

At that instant, Julie heard someone enter the room. It was a small man in janitorial clothing with a mop and water bucket. Something about the man's face seemed unnaturally kind, almost glowing.

"I have something to tell you," the man said softly. He took a step closer, his eyes locked on hers. "It's a message from God."

Julie's hands trembled and her mind raced. A message from God? Who was this man? He seemed like someone she'd known all her life.

"Your brother's going to be okay." The man winked at her. "Remember the words from Malachi 4:2." That said, he turned and left the room.

"Wait!" Julie jumped up and raced toward the door. Stepping into the hallway and expecting him to be a few feet away, she found an empty hallway with all the doors shut. How had he gotten away so fast? No one could move that quickly, especially with a bucket of water.

Julie waited a while, then headed for the nurses' desk. There was no way she could let the man get away without talking to him and finding out how he knew her brother or that he would live through the night.

But after she explained to the desk nurse what happened, the nurse replied, "All I can tell you, honey, is that all our janitors went home for the day, and we don't have a janitor who fits the description you gave."

With slow movements, Julie returned to the waiting room and began to pray again. *God, was that for me? That man . . . his message?* She exhaled hard and noticed her hands were shaking. Questions ricocheted in her soul until she heard someone enter the room . . . the doctor.

"Are your parents around?"

"They're in the cafeteria. How's Jared?"

A smile crossed the doctor's face. "It's nothing short of a miracle. Ten minutes ago, we thought we were losing him. Then he began coughing, and in a few minutes he was breathing normally again. We took an X-ray, and . . . I can't explain it. His lungs are dramatically better. I've never seen anything like it."

"You mean, he's okay?" Fresh tears filled Julie's eyes.

"He's out of danger. At least for now."

When Julie's parents returned, she shared the good news. The joy on their faces was instant, and she looked at them and said, "Can I tell you something? I think I saw an angel."

She told them the whole story, and for the first time they listened. And when they got home and read the Bible verse that spoke about revering God's name so that healing would come, her parents' attitude toward faith changed forever.

Seven years later, when Jared passed away from the cystic fibrosis, Julie said to the crowd of several hundred who came to his funeral, "My brother's entire life was a miracle. But it took a certain visitor one summer night to remind me that God was in control. My brother's in heaven now and his healing is complete." Then she looked up toward heaven, tears streaming down her face.

"I love you, Jared. Save me a spot at the lunch table."

Everyone born of God overcomes the

world. This is the victory that has overcome the world, even our faith.

1 JOHN 5:4

WEEK 49.
THE FIRST DAY OF
CHRISTMAS

SCRIPTURE READING:
2 KINGS 6:8–23

Have no fear of sudden disaster or of the ruin that overtakes the wicked, for the LORD will be your confidence and will keep your foot from being snared.

PROVERBS 3:25–26

Cara Wilcox was anxious to get out of the house for a while. It was December 12 — the first day of Christmas — and already the air was freezing cold outside. Life had been difficult for the Wilcox family lately and Cara had no idea how she'd afford Christmas. She knew the only way to get her mind off her worries was to get some fresh air.

It was very dark outside, and Cara's New York neighborhood was crowded and not very secure. She planned to walk no more than once around the block.

"Who wants to take a walk?" she asked as she pulled on her coat.

Sarah, five, and Joey, seven, shook their

305

heads and said, "We want to watch TV, Mom."

Her oldest son, Colin, fifteen, shrugged. "Not tonight, Mom. Okay?"

"Sure. But you watch Joey and Sarah. I'll take Laura."

Her three-year-old daughter had a lot of energy, and Cara picked up her riding toy. Even though it was cold, Cara could ride alongside her for one block without it bothering her. It would be good for both of them.

Once outside they had not traveled far when Laura no longer wanted her riding toy. Cara sighed and picked up the toy. As she did, she glanced behind her. She was only about half a block from home, and suddenly she saw Joey and Sarah walking up the street. They were acting sneaky, darting in and out of the shadows as if they were trying to catch up to their mother and surprise her, so Cara decided to play along.

She and Laura continued down the street until they reached the intersection. Cara turned around and looked for them again. This time she didn't see them.

"Hmm," she said, and Laura looked up at her.

"C'mon, Mommy. Walk."

Cara stood unmoving, staring back down

the block to see the children. Perhaps they had gotten scared of the dark and decided to go back home. Then the thought occurred to her that perhaps someone had snatched them. Crimes were committed around the neighborhood each day. Suddenly Cara began to panic.

"Sarah!" she called out. "Joey!"

There was no response and Cara could feel herself actually shaking in fear. She tightened her grip on Laura's hand and headed back toward the apartment.

As they walked, Cara noticed a man across the street who was headed in the same direction. She wondered where he had come from, since the few times she had looked back to check her children she hadn't noticed him. Although she was preoccupied with finding Joey and Sarah, Cara noticed that the man kept looking at them. Since she did not recognize him, she began to be suspicious and picked up her pace, sweeping Laura into her arms. In one hand she held the riding toy and decided she would use it in self-defense if necessary.

"What's wrong, Mommy?" Laura asked, aware of her mother's nervousness.

"Nothing, honey. We're going home now."

As Cara and her daughter neared the corner of her apartment building, the man began crossing the street at an angle headed in their direction. Terror raced through Cara's body, and she wondered if she could reach her apartment in time if he tried to accost them.

At that instant a thought came to Cara. *Pretend you see your father at the front door and talk to him,* a voice seemed to say. Instantly she acted on the suggestion.

"Hi, Dad!" Cara yelled, waving toward her apartment, still four units away. "Have you seen the kids?"

Almost at once the man who had been headed straight for her turned around and started walking in the opposite direction. Cara breathed a sigh of relief.

She ran up her apartment steps and dashed inside. Her fears alleviated, Cara saw Joey and Sarah on the floor watching television as they had been when she left.

"Why'd you guys come back home?" she asked.

The children looked blankly at their mother and then at each other. "What do you mean?" Joey asked.

"You were outside, following me. I saw you. Why'd you come back inside?"

Colin looked at his mother and shook his head. "Mom, they've been right here the whole time. They didn't want to go, remember?"

"That's impossible," she said. "I saw you both, following behind us. And when I couldn't see you anymore, I turned around."

Then Cara remembered the strange man. For the next fifteen minutes she tried to explain to Colin about the man and how threatened she had felt.

"Mom, maybe the kids you saw were angels and the only way they knew to get you to come back home was to make themselves look like Joey and Sarah. You know, Christmas angels."

Cara stared at her son. She had been thinking the same thing but was afraid she'd sound crazy. But why not? Wouldn't it have been fitting for God to use angels who looked like her kids? Her precious children.

"I don't know, son. But I'm sure I saw the kids outside tonight."

It wasn't until later that Cara came to believe without a doubt that a miracle had occurred. It turned out that the man who had been trailing her was an escaped felon. Until his recapture, he had been robbing people in Cara's neighborhood at gunpoint.

"God directed two children who looked just like mine to lead me back to safety while my children were inside the apartment the whole time," Cara told her friend later. "It was my Christmas miracle."

You are my hiding place; you will protect me from trouble and surround me with songs of deliverance.

PSALM 32:7

WEEK 50.
A CHARLIE BROWN
CHRISTMAS

SCRIPTURE READING:
NUMBERS 22:21–41

Do not be misled: "Bad company corrupts good character."

1 CORINTHIANS 15:33

Greg Jamison had always been popular at school. Tall with dark hair and blue eyes, he was handsome and athletic. Every sport he played came easily to him. The trouble was it all came too easily for him. Because of that he had stopped relying on God, stopped attending his parents' church, and almost stopped believing altogether.

During the week of Christmas break, Greg went to a handful of parties and started drinking beer — something he'd promised his parents he'd never do. He liked how it made him feel, especially with girls. After a week of drinking, he was asked to a party to try pot.

"All right, cool. See ya there." Greg's stomach churned the moment he heard himself say the words.

On the night of the party, his mother said, "You've been out too much this week, Greg. Stay home tonight. We're watching 'A Charlie Brown Christmas.' "

A twinge of regret pierced Greg's heart. This had been his favorite holiday program. "I'm too old for that. And I'm too old to stay home."

"Watch your tone, son," his father joined in. "As long as you're living under our roof you need to show a little more respect."

Greg had uttered a few apologies and dashed out the door. He spent the next hour driving the roads near his home in Wichita, wondering what was happening to his life. What would his parents think? If the coaches heard what he'd been doing, he'd be cut from the team.

And what about God? If there was a God, then Greg was in big trouble. But what if there was no God? What if you died and were no more?

The questions swirled through Greg's mind. If he went to the party, he could forget about it. A few drugs wouldn't hurt him, would they?

He was about to head toward the party when he saw what looked like a prison guard hitchhiking along the side of the road. The prison was about ten miles down the road, so it made sense.

Greg pulled over. The man's eyes were a kind, gentle brown and his smile looked harmless.

"Need a ride?"

"Thanks. I was hoping you'd stop."

"You work at the prison?"

"For the past ten years. Shift starts in five minutes."

"Get in." Greg unlocked the door.

As the man climbed inside, Greg saw he was in his fifties, with graying hair and a mustache. Somehow his face had a glow about it, even in the dark. His prison guard uniform was perfectly pressed.

"What's your name?"

"Ralph Michaels."

Greg was silent a moment. The man seemed unusually calm and relaxed, considering he was late for work and having to hitchhike for some reason.

The prison guard turned toward him. "Now, why don't you tell me what's on your mind?"

Greg was unsure what to make of the man, but he started telling him about school.

"No. Tell me about the crossroad."

Greg stared at the man, wondering how he could know to ask such a question.

"What do you mean?"

"You know what I mean. You have some choices you're trying to make, don't you?"

Greg felt strangely uncomfortable, as if the man could read his thoughts. Still, Greg felt like talking, so he began to tell the man the truth. He told him about his spiritual upbringing. "But I'm different now; that kind of life is in my past."

"No. That kind of life is closer than you think."

"What would you know about it?"

"I do know." The man spoke with a finality that set Greg on edge.

"Look . . . I don't know who you are, but yeah, I'm at a crossroads. I've been good all my life and now I want to find some things out for myself."

The man stared straight ahead for several minutes before turning toward Greg. "There's only one right way."

"Look, I'm tired of talking." The prison had just appeared on their right. "Where can I drop you off?"

"This is fine." He turned toward Greg. "Make the right choice. Now. You still have the chance." He climbed out and paused. "Besides . . . 'A Charlie Brown Christmas' isn't so bad, is it, Greg?"

"No. . . ."

The man winked. "I didn't think so." Then he turned and headed up the long driveway toward the prison.

As Greg pulled away he was stunned. How had the guard known his name? Or about the Charlie Brown special? Greg suddenly wanted nothing more than to go back home and watch the movie.

Into the next morning Greg thought over everything the man had said. He decided he needed to talk to the man again. He called the prison and spoke to a supervisor who spent ten minutes convincing Greg that there never had been a Ralph Michaels employed at the prison. And that all the guards working the previous night were in their twenties.

Stunned, Greg told his parents about the encounter.

"Sometimes God gets our attention in interesting ways," his mother said. "He might have been an angel."

"An angel?" Greg felt his heartbeat double.

"Why not? God is still God, and his ways aren't so different now than they were back in Bible times."

For several weeks Greg considered the possibility, until finally he was convinced that his mother was right. He decided he would no longer involve himself in parties and began attending church again. He found a peace and assurance he had never believed could exist.

My lord has wisdom like that of an angel of God — he knows everything that happens in the land.

2 SAMUEL 14:20

WEEK 51.
A HELPING HAND

SCRIPTURE READING:
2 KINGS 4:1–7

My God will meet all your needs according to his glorious riches in Christ Jesus.
PHILIPPIANS 4:19

Adam Armstrong received the call just after nine on Christmas Day while on patrol with the sheriff's department in Akron, Ohio. A woman was weeping loudly at a truck stop on the highway outside of town.

A veteran officer of eight years, Armstrong had seen so much pain in people's lives that he could only imagine what might cause a woman to weep aloud in a truck stop, especially on Christmas evening. As he drove, he remembered this was the reason he joined the police force in the first place. He had ridden along with a police officer as part of the research for a local newspaper story he was writing. The first call involved a woman who had been badly beaten by her husband. As the officer led the man away, he saw the relief on the woman's face, and

317

suddenly something clicked. He might write a thousand stories about good and evil in the course of a lifetime. But no story could ever rescue that woman from her pain as the police officer had.

Armstrong sought police work the very next day and never once looked back. Despite the danger and frustration that came with the job, his love for his work was as strong as it had been in the beginning.

He entered the truck stop café — aglow with Christmas lights — and spotted the woman, her face covered with her hands. Nearby sat two frightened little blonde girls who seemed to be around four and five years old.

"What seems to be the matter, girls?" he asked. The older child looked up, and Armstrong saw the tears.

"Daddy couldn't get us no Christmas presents, so he left us here."

Armstrong's heart sank. He smiled at the girls. "In that case I want you two to climb on those stools over there and order something to eat."

Reluctantly the girls walked away from their mother and took separate stools along the counter. Armstrong told the waitress to get the girls whatever they wanted.

With the children out of earshot, he sat

down across from the woman. She stared sadly at Armstrong, her eyes filled with heartbreak.

"What's the problem?" he asked quietly.

"It's what my girl said," the woman replied, wiping her eyes. "My husband's at the end of his rope. We're flat broke, and he figured we'd get more help alone than if he stayed. I've been sitting here praying about what to do next. It hasn't been a very good Christmas, sir." Fresh tears appeared. "I just want to know God is listening."

Armstrong nodded, his eyes gentle and empathetic. And silently he added his own prayer. *She needs an angel about now, Lord. Please help her out.*

"Do you have family?"

"The nearest is in Tulsa."

Armstrong suggested several agencies that could help her. As they spoke, the waitress brought hot dogs and French fries to the children, so he stood up and moved toward the counter, taking out his wallet.

"The boss says no charge," the waitress said.

Armstrong smiled at the woman and nodded his thanks. As he did, a trucker approached the waitress. He said something to her, then she led him to Armstrong.

Typically truck drivers and police officers

have something of a natural animosity for one another. Armstrong couldn't remember a time when he'd been approached by a truck driver outside the line of duty.

The trucker walked up and stood alongside him. Armstrong noticed that the normal buzz of activity had stilled and the café was silent. Most of the patrons — nearly all long-distance truckers — were watching.

"Excuse me, Officer. Here," the trucker said as he handed Armstrong a fistful of bills. "We passed the hat. There ought to be enough to get the woman and her girls started on their way."

When he was young, Armstrong had learned that cops don't cry in public. So he stood there, speechless until the lump in his throat disappeared, then he shook the man's hand firmly. "I'm sure she'll appreciate it. Can I tell her your name?"

"Nope. Just tell her it's from folks with families of their own who wish they were home for Christmas, too."

As the trucker walked away, Armstrong counted the money and was again amazed. A small room of truck drivers had in a matter of minutes raised two hundred dollars, enough money for three bus tickets to Tulsa and food along the way.

He walked back to the booth and handed

the money to the woman, at which point she began to sob again.

"He heard," she whispered through her tears.

"Ma'am?" Armstrong was confused.

"Don't you see?" she said. "I asked God to give us a sign that he still loved us and cared for us."

Armstrong felt chills along his arms and remembered his own prayer for angelic assistance. The truck drivers didn't look like a textbook group of angels, but God had used them all the same. "You know, ma'am, I think he really did hear."

At that instant, a young couple approached the sobbing woman and asked if they could help in any way.

"Well, we could use a ride. . . ."

Armstrong walked discreetly away from the scene and radioed dispatch. "The situation's resolved."

Not until he drove away from the café did Armstrong let the tears come. He almost always saw the worst in people. But that night, he'd been reminded that kindness and love do exist among men. And he learned that sometimes God answered prayer using bighearted truckers to play the part of Christmas angels.

Glory to God in the highest, and on earth
peace to men on whom his favor rests.

LUKE 2:14

Week 52.
Forgiven All Along

SCRIPTURE READING:
2 SAMUEL 11

If we confess our sins, he is faithful and just and will forgive us our sins and purify us from all unrighteousness.

1 JOHN 1:9

Penny Hathaway had big dreams as a teenager. She wanted to spend a year with her actress aunt in Chicago and a year in New York City, before attending the University of Southern California as a film major. Penny thought she'd suffocate if she didn't get out of her small town.

Her senior year, Penny worked at a restaurant, saving her tips and wages toward her trip. The day before she left, her parents told her, "God has a plan for your life, Penny. Seek after that."

Penny felt her parents' faith was stifling, enough to squeeze the life out of her creativity. Part of living an artist's life was expressing one's passions, right? But Penny only nodded and smiled.

Chicago life was everything Penny had dreamed. She got a job at a five-star steak restaurant and struck up a friendship with her free-spirited aunt, who had only one rule: if you play around, don't get caught.

She met a dashing young man, Adrian, who had a role in one of the big theater productions. He was handsome and talented and showed her around backstage and introduced her to the cast. Later, he took her to his apartment and introduced her to champagne. When he wanted to sleep with her that night, Penny said yes. This was part of her new life: passion without restrictions.

The pattern between them continued for the next two months, but deep inside Penny felt the stirrings of panic. Her period was three weeks late, and she heard Adrian was seeing another girl. When she confronted him, he laughed. "In my world people explore each other. Sometimes one person at a time, sometimes more."

She bought an early pregnancy test the next morning. It took less than ten minutes to confirm her suspicions: she was pregnant. When she told Adrian, he said, "Well, I'm sure you'll figure something out." It was the last time he sought her out.

Having thrown faith and morals out the window, everything Penny had been warned about had happened. Finally, when she was ten weeks pregnant, she determined to turn her life around. She contacted an adoption attorney and explained what she wanted to do. The adoption would be closed, he told her. No contact until the child reached eighteen, and then only if he or she looked into the files.

Penny agreed to the terms and later gave birth to a healthy baby boy. She held him for fifteen minutes, awestruck over his perfect features and full head of dark hair. He would be artistic, handsome, and tall like his father, sensitive and curious like her.

But the minute the baby was taken away, somewhere deep within Penny's heart a seed of guilt took root. How would her son feel about her when he was old enough to realize what she'd done? Yet she thought she'd made the right choice.

As the years passed, Penny marked her son's birthdays, imagining what he might be like at various ages. Rather than diminish, the guilt intensified with time. Six years later she graduated from USC and told her parents about the baby. They agreed that adoption had been the best choice.

More years passed and Penny joined a church. There she grew closer to God, certain that her earlier mistakes were forgiven. Eventually she met a kind business-man, someone who shared her love of God and the arts. They married and began a life of their own. But still, voices haunted her. Where was her son? Did he hate her?

When Penny miscarried their first child, she wept for days, wondering if God was punishing her. Never mind that the women's minister at her church told her that adoption was clearly the kindest option. She still felt like an awful mother, even after she had three children with her husband.

As seventeen years passed she knew only one thing could ease her guilt — hearing from her son himself that he was happy. Her only hope was to write a letter and have it put in his file. She told him all that had happened and of her deep regrets. "I did what I thought was best for you. But I won't have peace until I hear you've read my apology." Penny sent the letter, prayed, and waited.

Her son turned eighteen and then nineteen; still she worried and wondered. Then, after her son's twentieth birthday, Penny received a hand-addressed letter from a Jeremy Bennett. Tears blurred her eyes from the opening words that told her he was indeed her son.

These were the words she had longed to read: "Penny, I have had a wonderful life.

My parents are loving Christians who have raised me to believe in God, hard work, and family. I plan to attend medical school. . . . I want to put your mind at ease, and I want to thank you. Giving me up for adoption was the most loving thing you could have done for me. Don't worry for one minute that you made a wrong choice. I will always be grateful."

Penny closed her eyes and raised her face to the heavens, feeling almost as if she were standing on holy ground. God had worked a miracle, replacing a lifetime of guilt and doubt with a peace that would last for all time.

A month later she met Jeremy for herself and saw in his eyes that everything he'd told her was true. And God gave her something else: an hour-long concert, compliments of her son, the medical student with an uncanny love for the arts.

I, even I, am he who blots out your transgressions, for my own sake, and remembers your sins no more.

ISAIAH 43:25

327

ABOUT THE AUTHOR

Bestselling author **Karen Kingsbury** is America's #1 inspirational novelist. She's written more than forty novels, ten of which have hit #1 on bestseller lists. Her Center Street novel *This Side of Heaven* stayed on the *New York Times* bestseller list for several weeks. She lives in Washington State with her husband, Don, and their six children, three of whom are adopted from Haiti.